NIGERIA

THE LAND, ITS ART AND ITS PEOPLE

AN ANTHOLOGY
Edited by Frederick Lumley

Photographs by Werner Forman

STUDIO VISTA

*The walls of Kano, part of the
ancient fortification.*

First published in Great Britain in 1974 by Studio Vista, a division of Cassell & Collier
Macmillan Publishers Ltd., London, 35 Red Lion Square, London WC1R 4SG, Sydney,
Auckland, Toronto, Johannesburg, an affiliate of Macmillan Publishing Co. Inc.,
New York.

Printed in Great Britain by BAS Printers Limited, Wallop, Hampshire and bound by
Kemp Hall Bindery, Oxford.

ISBN 0 289 70488 X

List of Contents

Bronze plate from the Palace of the Oba of Benin, representing the Oba's drummer.

INTRODUCTION

THESE pages aim to capture the spirit and ethos of a nation, Nigeria, its people and its places. As such, this anthology becomes a microcosm of different families—Hausa, Fulani, Yoruba, Ibo, Kanuri, Ibibio, Effik, Tiv and Birom to name some of the leading members—which make up the teeming population of a country as old as the pre-history of Africa and as new as a nation which achieved independence on 1 October 1960. The sweep of our canvas presents an emphasis on youth at a crucial moment of its history, looking forward and looking back. Any attempt to view in perspective the conflux of past and present reminds us that the heritage of Nigeria takes us back long before the Portuguese and the peoples of the Niger delta 'discovered' each other, to the first millenium for which sources are either archaelogical or rely on the oral tradition of legends passed from generation to generation.

There follows the period of 'the interlopers', the Europeans, whether they came for exploration or to exploit the slave trade, which reached its peak in the eighteenth century. With the nineteenth century we find some Europeans with more altruistic motives, wishing to extend to the different Nigerian tribes the benefits of European knowledge, morality and civilization which seemed destined to conquer the world. It was only in our present century, after the savagery of two world wars, that a profound pessimism and pragmatic considerations led European powers to accept the necessity of decolonization.

No colonial administration could ever have envisaged perhaps the greatest legacy the British offered the young Nigerian elite; the English language. Almost coinciding with the handing over of power, young Nigerian writers—poets, novelists and playwrights—began to attract attention. While some of them still preferred Yoruba and other languages, the majority of them had chosen English, though like all writers of value, they achieved their international reputations through their indigenous nationalism. Like Nigeria's leaders and technocrats, they share the accent of youth. While it was not possible for them to become full-time writers in Nigeria without a job, nearly all have posts in government employment, the media, or in the universities. Yet in spite of this, or perhaps because this brings them into closer touch with the people, their writing captures the different facets of Nigerian life with an innocent originality which is a rare commodity in the hurly-burly of Western publishing. It seems that one writer tends to stimulate another, and as in a golden age, standards rise, while at the same time the diversity of Nigerian authors defies any academic attempt at classification, or to call them a 'Nigerian school'. The extremes of sophistication of city lights mingle with the labyrinthine shades and spirits of Amos Tutuola. It is as if they have added a further rule of the road to drivers: beware at all times of ghosts.

Confronted with this galaxy of talent, the problem has been one of selection. The cross-currents of tradition meet the shock of modernity, with a surprising result that instead of forming a symbiosis, the two stretch complementary to one another. The diversity of subjects has unfortunately prevented the inclusion of many names one would have liked to have introduced, and even the selected passages of individual authors in many cases do not suggest the diversity of their own writing. I regret, in particular, that it has not been possible to include excerpts from plays (where to do justice passages might have required a complete act) and the name of Wole Soyinka is represented here only as a poet and novelist, although he has become one of the major dramatists of our time. There are also many authors who would have merited a place had this anthology restricted itself to purely contemporary Nigerian authors. I have sought to depict an atmosphere of place rather than show the more universal problems of conflict between urban and rural communities. The choice inevitably reflects a personal viewpoint from the outside, but what is important is that this anthology should encourage readers to discover for themselves the range and depth of Nigerian literature.

A country can only be understood, I believe, in relation to its past, and here I have relied mainly on European narrators, with the exception of Olaudah Equiano, an Ibo born around 1745, and Baba of Karo, an old Hausa woman's memories of life at the turn of the century. In the company of Captain Clapperton, Major Dixon Denham, Richard Lander, and Messrs Allen and Thomson it would be pleasant to while away some evenings in a London Club listening to accounts of their expeditions; however, with the congenial bravado of Sir Richard Burton, a figure smitten with Wanderlust from childhood, one would willingly have shared his experiences as he wandered across the continents, India, Arabia, America, or took part in the expedition with Speke to discover the sources of the Nile, or explored the West African coast. Finally there is the feminine charm of Mary Kingsley, no mere tourist, but one of the first Europeans to study African societies from within, and to look forward, in an age of Victorian imperialism, to what she called 'the African principle' that Africans should be governed by Africans.

We require an Einsteinian imagination to break the time barrier between the death of Mungo Park in 1806 and that of Nigeria's great poet Christopher Okigbo on the Nsukka battlefield in 1967, and span the centuries so that the present becomes a mere cog that links the past with the future and momentarily releases the four dimensions of reality. As such the rancour of the past merges with the spirits of the forest, and before us lies an etherial early morning mist which has to clear to reveal the future. Nigeria has become a landfall for the creative vision, for whom the present is like the flash of a camera, the visual eye of the objective reporter or the creative mystic and poet which I hope these pages convey.

Frederick Lumley

INDEPENDENCE

Adebayo Faleti

Translated from the Yoruba by Bakare Gbadamosi and Ulli Beier.

There is nothing as sweet as independence.
It is a great day on which the slave buys his freedom.
When a slave can go to fetch water
And nobody can tell him: you are coming late!
When a slave will fetch firewood
And use it to cook his own food!
When a slave can bring home a couple of yams
Everyday, to use for his meal.
When the slave does not serve anybody,
When he is merely serving himself!
What a day, when the slave wakes up to rest—
Not to go to another man's farm!
When the slave starts planting his own farm.
Four hundred and twenty rows of yam!
When he will plant the maize and dig the yam.
When he will sell his crop and use it for his own family.
No longer will he do unpaid work.
No longer waste his old age serving others.
The slave will rejoice, rejoice, rejoice.
He will jump up into the air and slap his body with his arms.
He will sing the song and say:
'Help me to be thankful I am lucky!'
Let us rejoice with the slave.
The one whose life has never been pawned
Does not know the hardship of work before dawn.
A person who has never been a slave
Does not know the hardship of the stable boy.
He will never know what it means
To brush the dew off the leaves in the morning
And stay on the farm until after dark—slicing yams.
In the dry season or in the rainy season—
There is no escape from it.
The eyes of the slave have seen many things.
If a man's life is pawned
And he is as tall as the Ogun tree in the king's market,
He is as small as a dwarf terrier in the eyes of his master.
And if the master is burnt out like an old stick,
And if he is mangy like a scruffy old dog,
He will still be acting like the master.

A fireman of Ibadan in front of the University, where he is enrolled as a student.

15

The Oba's drummer during the Yam Festival.

The eyes of the slave have seen everything!
No day is like the day when the elephant served under the duiker.
Duiker sent elephant to the river,
But elephant did not return in time.
Duiker beat elephant.
Duiker abused elephant on the bridge.
He reminded elephant that he was rich enough to own him.
But the elephant accepted the punishment with love.
He said: it is not because I am stupid,
Or because I have not grown up.
If the slave moves carefully,
He may still buy his freedom after a long, long time.
It was not too late for the elephant
To buy himself free and become the head of the animals.
Let us learn wisdom from the elephant.
Let us shake off our suffering with patience.
Gently we kill the fly on our own body.
Let all of us get ready to buy ourselves back!
After all: we have land, and we have hoes.
We have cocoa trees and we have bananas.
We have palm kernels and we have groundnuts.
Let us fight, so that we may cultivate our own farm.
To escape from being slaves and pawns,
Let all our people be free.

Mr. M. Park.

MAPPING THE NIGER

Downing-street, 2 January 1805.

Sir,

It being judged expedient that a small expedition should be sent into the interior of Africa, with a view to discover and ascertain whether any, and what commercial intercourse can be opened therein for the mutual benefit of the natives and of His Majesty's subjects.

When you shall have prepared whatever may be necessary for securing the objects of your expedition at Goree, you are to proceed up the river Gambia; and thence crossing over to the Senegal to march by such route as you shall find most eligible, to the banks of the Niger.

The great object of your journey will be to pursue the course of this river to the utmost possible distance to which it can be traced; to establish communication and intercourse with the different nations on the banks; to obtain all the local knowledge in your power respecting them.

I am &c.
Camden.

To Mungo Park, Esq.

THE MISSING JOURNAL OF MUNGO PARK

Richard Lander

18 June . . . This morning we visited the far-famed Niger or Quorra, which flows by the city, and were greatly disappointed at the appearance of this celebrated river. Black, rugged rocks rose abruptly from the centre of the stream. The Niger here, in its widest part, is not more than a stone's throw across at present. The rock on which we sat overlooks the spot where Mr Park and his associates met their unhappy fate.

19 June . . . the king, accompanied by his consort, who is said to be his counsellor and only confidant, honoured us with a visit at our hut. They came without any kind of state or ceremony, and were both dressed more plainly than many of their subjects. The queen is the daughter of the last and sister of the present ruler of Wowow.

The demand for coral has been very great in every town of consequence which we have visited. All ranks of people appear passionately fond of wearing it, and it is preferred to every other ornament whatever. The midikie asked us, this morning, if we had brought any coral with us, and seemed rather disappointed, though not displeased, on being answered in the negative. She then pulled out a little box, made of sheep skin, which was filled with coral beads and little golden trinkets, and requested me to polish the latter for her. We offered her a few plated buttons, which we had just before been cleaning, and they were accepted with transport; but as their brightness had excited the admiration of her consort, a scramble took place as to which of the two should have them. After a long struggle, it ended in the triumph of the king, who first chose the largest and best for his own use, and then gave his spouse the remainder. The royal couple were like two great children, yet they were each well pleased with their own, and expressed their thankfulness with much warmth.

We imagined that it would have been bad policy to have stated the true reason for our visiting this country, knowing the jealousy of most of the people with regard to the Niger; and, therefore, in answer to the king's inquiries, I was obliged to deceive him with the assertion that our object was to go to Bornou by way of Yaoorie, requesting at the same time a safe conveyance through his territories. This answer satisfied the king, and he promised us every assistance in his power. Our visitors remained with us a considerable time, and in the course of conversation, one of them observed that they had in their possession a tobe, which belonged to a white man who came from the north many years ago, and from whom it had been purchased by the king's father.

A river landscape from Park's Travels. The bearded figure on the right was supposed to be Mungo Park.

We expressed great curiosity to see this tobe, and it was sent us as a present a short time after their departure. Contrary to our expectations, we found it to be made of rich crimson damask, and very heavy from the immense quantity of gold embroidery with which it was covered. As the time when the late king is said to have purchased this tobe corresponds very nearly to the supposed period of Mr Park's death, and as we have never heard of any other white man having come from the north so far south as Boossa, we are inclined to believe it to be part of the spoil obtained from the canoe of that ill-fated traveller.

Sunday, 20 June. Eager as we are to obtain even the slightest information relative to the unhappy fate of Mr Park and his companions, as well as to ascertain if any of their books or papers are now in existence at this place, we had almost made up our minds to refrain from asking any questions on the subject, because we were apprehensive that it might be displeasing to the king, and involve us in many perplexities. Familiarity, however, having in some measure worn off this impression, and the king being an affable, obliging, and good-natured person, we were emboldened to send Paskoe to him this morning, with a message expressive of the interest we felt on the subject, in common with all our countrymen; and saying that, if any books or papers which belonged to Mr Park were yet in his possession, he would do us a great service,

'The Palaver' based on Captain William Allen's sketches describing a deputation which visited Lander to assure him of a king's friendly intentions.

'They often wear a striped blue and cotton cloth round the waist or thrown in various graceful ways over the shoulder; and there is some art in arranging the folds, so that it shall not fall off. Indeed, they frequently remind me of the manner in which some of the best statues of antiquity are draped.'

by delivering them into our hands, or at least by granting us permission to see them. To this the king returned for answer that when Mr Park was lost in the Niger, he was a very little boy, and that he knew not what had become of his effects; that the deplorable event had occurred in the reign of the late king's predecessor, who died shortly after; and that all traces of the white man had been lost with him. This answer disappointed our hopes, for to us it appeared final and decisive. But in the evening they were again raised by a hint from our host, who is the king's drummer, and one of the principal men in the country; he assured us, that there was certainly one book at least saved from Mr Park's canoe, which is now in the possession of a very poor man in the service of his master, to whom it had been entrusted by the late king during his last illness. He said moreover, that if but one application were made to the king, on any subject whatever, very little was thought of it; but if a second were made, the matter would be considered of sufficient importance to demand his whole attention—such being the custom of the country. . . . At his own request, we sent him to the king immediately, desiring him to repeat our former statement, and to assure the king, that should he be successful in recovering the book we wanted, our monarch would reward him handsomely. He desired the drummer to inform us, that he would examine the man who was reported to have the white man's book in his possession, at an early hour tomorrow.

21 June. The city of Boossa consists of a great number of groups or clusters of huts, all within a short distance of each other. It is bounded one side by the river Niger, and on the other by an extensive turreted wall, with moats, forming a complete semi-circle. Notwithstanding, however, its natural and artificial defences, Boossa was taken by the Falatahs many years ago; on which occasion its inhabitants fled, with their children and effects, to one of the little islands in the Niger. But the chiefs of Niki, Wowow, and Kiama, having been made acquainted with the circumstance, and having joined their forces with those of Boossa, drove the Falatahs, their common enemy, into the Niger, where many of them perished. Since that period the city has never been invaded, nor threatened with attack. The soil of Boossa is, for the most part, very fertile, and produces rice, corn, yams, etc., in great abundance. Very good salt is brought from a salt lake on the borders of the river, which is about ten days' journey to the northward of this place. Guinea-fowl, pheasants, partridges, and a variety of aquatic birds are found here in the greatest plenty, and have afforded us excellent sport. Deer and antelope also abound near the city; but they are timid and shy, and rarely, if ever, caught by the inhabitants. The fish, with which this river abounds so plentifully, are eaten by all classes of people: they are tough, dry, and unsavoury; yet they form part of the daily food of the inhabitants, who appear exceedingly fond of them.

The Hausa language is understood by the generality of the natives of Borgoo, almost as well as their mother-tongue, and it is spoken by the majority of them with considerable fluency. The government of the country is despotic; but this unlimited power, which is vested in the monarch, is almost invariably exercised with lenity and forbearance. All private disputes are settled by the king, and he punishes misdemeanours just as his inclination may lead him.

In the afternoon, the king came to see us, followed by a man with a book under his arm, which was said to have been picked up in the Niger after the loss of our countryman. It was enveloped in a large cotton cloth, and our hearts beat high with expectation as the man was slowly unfolding it, for by its size we guessed it to be Mr Park's journal; but our disappointment and chagrin were great, when, on opening the book, we discovered it to be an old nautical publication of the last century. The title page was missing, but its contents were chiefly tables of logarithms. It was a thick royal quarto; between the leaves we found a few loose pages of very little consequence indeed; one of them contained two or three observations on the height of the water in the Gambia; one was a tailor's bill on a Mr Anderson; and another was addressed to Mr Mungo Park, and contained an invitation to dinner—the following is a copy of it:

'Mr and Mrs Watson would be happy to have the pleasure of Mr Park's company at dinner on Tuesday next, at half-past five o'clock.
'An answer is requested.

'Strand, 9 Nov. 1804.'

The king, as well as the owner of the book, looked as greatly mortified as ourselves, when they were told that the one produced was not that of which we were in quest, because the reward promised would not of course be obtained. As soon as our curiosity had been fully satisfied, the papers were carefully collected and placed again between the leaves, and the book as carefully folded in its envelope as before, and taken away by its owner, who values it much as a household god.

THE BISHOP OF THE NIGER

Adolf Burdo

'This morning,' he said, 'the Bishop of the Niger was informed by a fisherman that there was a white man in these parts. He has sent me to you to ask if you are in need of help; he places his house at your disposal, and offers you hospitality.'

Words fail me to describe what passed in my mind at that moment. Those only who have experienced the revulsion from terrible distress to unmixed joy can imagine the emotion with which I listened to these words. But an hour ago everything seemed to be irretrievably lost, and now most unexpectedly, all was restored. It was the name of the Bishop of the Niger which had worked this miracle.

Having thanked my interlocutor, I asked him to help me in settling accounts with my rowers: he kindly undertook it, and having dismissed them he replaced them by four others who were stationed on the shore.

'These men,' said he, 'will take care of your effects; they are known to me and you may place confidence in them. Now come with me, I will take you to the bishop.'

The mission station is situated at the foot of Mount Patteh, below the negro village. On coming from the south you cross the course of a small stream, which the rains sometimes change into a torrent, while at others it is quite dry. A few trees have been thrown over it, by way of precaution, for a bridge. The mission occupies a large square, enclosed by a wall of hardened sand, and consists of a suite of rooms for the use of the bishop, another for his servants, and another—a prolongation of these—which serves as a kitchen. At the lower part of the quadrangle, a modest building was in progress and about half finished, intended for a church. All this, it must be explained, is of the very simplest description; one storey, no windows, gravel floor—this was all. Nevertheless, it seemed to me when I lifted the mat that did duty for a door and entered this hospitable abode, that I was crossing the threshold of a palace.

'You are welcome, sir,' said a native with white hair, to me in English, clad in a long black frock coat and trousers of the same colour. This was Samuel Ajai Crowther, Bishop of the Niger.

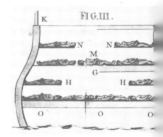

*

The Bishop of the Niger was born in Igbira-Panda on the Benueh. As I have said, there is nothing in the slightest degree resembling our registration system, so that he does not know his precise age; but his grey head suggests that he may be about fifty.

He remembers scarcely anything of his earliest years; it may be supposed, however, that his father was one of the dignitaries of the tribe, for unlike the lower orders of the people, the traditions and sentiment of the family had been preserved in the hut in which he first saw the light.

One morning, when he might have been about nine years old, all the tribe ran in terror to arms. Numerous bands had rushed upon the village: there was a terrible fight, and the assailants gained the victory.

It was one of the slave hunts that the child had just witnessed, carried on by the Fulanis. The Fulanis, who are negro Mussulmans, have by degrees invaded all the right shore of the Benueh, sacking the villages, cutting the throats of all the old men and women, massacring all who resisted them, and dragging away in their train the men, women, girls, and children to sell them at the Eastern markets or on the coast.

The future Bishop of the Niger saw his father killed before his eyes. He clung to his mother's knees; but the Fulanis dragged him away, leaving the poor woman insensible on the threshold of the hut which was reduced to ashes.

For a whole year the child was taken from one market to another without finding a purchaser. What he suffered during these long peregrinations, and the atrocities he witnessed, are known to none but God and himself.

He was taken at length to the Western coast, and sold to some Portuguese slave-traders. The brig in which he embarked was one of those which they called a tomb; it was a clipper with a double deck. The slaves were stowed away in the hold as a cargo of ebony; in case of pursuit by a French or English cruiser, they were taken in chains to the false deck in the fore part of the vessel, and at a given signal were plunged by means of machinery into the water. After this precaution the slaveship could be boarded without fear; it appeared like a respectable merchantman.

Cross-section through a slave ship from An Essay in Colonization *by C. B. Wadstrom published in London in 1794.*

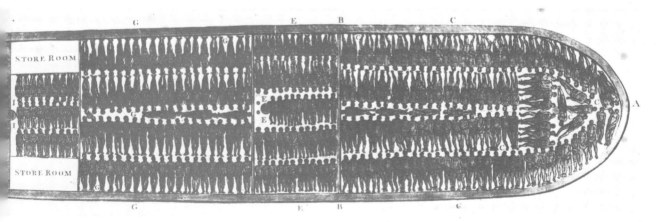

My son! My son! A contemporary illustration from Burdo's The Bishop of the Niger.

Having left Old Calabar without let or hindrance, near St Helena the vessel with our young negro on board was chased by an English cruiser. Having no hope of escape, the trader thought to get out of the difficulty by throwing his cargo of human flesh into the sea.

In the dire confusion on board the slaver, occasioned by the approach of the cruiser, the child succeeded in hiding between two bags of salt.

The English boarded the vessel; they had seen the trader's game, and the punishment was not long to follow; the traders in human flesh were hung to the highest yards, and the clipper was to be sunk. But before sinking her they went over her.

Thus the child was saved. Touched with compassion, the English officers took him to Sierra Leone, where he was put to school. He made such rapid progress that it was thought he ought to be sent to London to finish his studies; there he conceived a desire for the ministry, was ordained and by his own request was sent to the coast of Africa as a missionary. He distinguished himself there by his courage, his aptitude and zeal, and rendered so many services to the cause of civilization and the scientific enterprises with which he was associated, that in 1864 he was recalled to England, and consecrated bishop by the Archbishop of Canterbury; it was then that the Upper Niger was assigned to him as his diocese, and he returned thither to evangelize his compatriots.

One day, when he was preaching at Imaha, a large village of Igbira-Panda, a poor old woman, bowed down with age and sorrows, drew near the group of natives formed round the black pastor. All at once the poor old creature is seized with trembling; the preacher's voice strikes her ear; she tries to see him, but the natives hide him from her. She listens again—suddenly, as if some infatuation had seized her, she makes way for herself through the crowd, and half dead throws her arms round the bishop, exclaiming, 'My son! my son!' It was indeed his mother, whom the traders did not care to take, and who, left for dead, after having seen her son torn away, had thus escaped both butchery and slavery. For eight-and-twenty years she had been wandering from village to village in quest of her son. She had just found him as a bishop.

While the good man was narrating this episode of his life, large tears coursed down his cheeks. 'If,' added he, 'I have done any good here, I was rewarded for it a hundred fold by this moment of ineffable bliss.' He took his old mother to Lagos, where he had taken up his abode, and surrounded her with all the care, the kindness, and tenderness, which her life had hitherto been without, and closed her eyes himself when a few years ago she expired in his arms.

Such is this good man, Samuel Agai Crowther, Bishop of the Niger, and he is to this day one of the most vigilant propagators of civilization in Central Africa.

MY IBO HOMELAND

Olaudah Equiano

That part of Africa, known by the name of Guinea, to which the trade for slaves is carried on, extends along the coast above 3,400 miles, from Senegal to Angola, and includes a variety of kingdoms. Of these the most considerable is the kingdom of Benin, both as to extent and wealth, the richness and cultivation of the soil, the power of its king, and the number and warlike disposition of the inhabitants. It is situated nearly under the line, and extends along the coast about 170 miles, but runs back into the interior part of Africa, to a distance hitherto I believe unexplored by any traveller; and seems only terminated at length by the empire of Abyssinia, near 1,500 miles from its beginning. This kingdom is divided into many provinces or districts: in one of the most remote and fertile of which I was born, in the year 1745, situated in a charming fruitful vale, named Essaka. The distance of this province from the capital of Benin and the sea coast must be very considerable; for I had never heard of white men or Europeans, nor of the sea; and our subjection to the king of Benin was little more than nominal; for every transaction of the government, as far as my slender observation extended, was conducted by the chiefs or elders of the place. The manners and government of a people who have little commerce with other countries are generally very simple; and the history of what passes in one family or village, may serve as a specimen of the whole nation. My father was one of those elders or chiefs I have spoken of, and was styled Embrenché; a term, as I remember, importing the highest distinction, and signifying in our language a mark of grandeur. This mark is conferred on the person entitled to it, by cutting the skin across at the top of the forehead, and drawing it down to the eyebrows;

Bronze head from Ife, c. 1000–1200 AD.

and, while it is in this situation, applying a warm hand, and rubbing it until it shrinks up into a thick weal across the lower part of the forehead. Most of the judges and senators were thus marked; my father had long borne it: I had seen it conferred on one of my brothers, and I also was destined to receive it by my parents. Those Embrenché, or chief men, decided disputes, and punished crimes; for which purpose they always assembled together. The proceedings were generally short; and in most cases the law of retaliation prevailed. . . .

We are almost a nation of dancers, musicians, and poets. Thus every great event, such as a triumphant return from battle, or other cause of public rejoicing, is celebrated in public dances, which are accompanied with songs and music suited to the occasion. The assembly is separated into four divisions, which dance either apart or in succession, and each with a character peculiar to itself. The first division contains the married men, who, in their dances, frequently exhibit feats of arms, and the representation of a battle. To these succeed the married women, who dance in the second division. The young men occupy the third; and the maidens the fourth. Each represents some interesting scene of real life, such as a great achievement, domestic employment, a pathetic story, or some rural sport; and, as the subject is generally founded on some recent event, it is therefore ever new. This gives our dances a spirit and variety which I have scarcely seen elsewhere. We have many musical instruments, particularly drums of different kinds, a piece of music which resembles a guitar, and another much like a stickado. These last are chiefly used by betrothed virgins, who play on them on all grand festivals.

Brass wire ornaments worn by Ibo women, from a nineteenth-century engraving.

As our manners are simple, our luxuries are few. The dress of both sexes is nearly the same. It generally consists of a long piece of calico, or muslin, wrapped loosely round the body, somewhat in the form of a highland plaid. This is usually dyed blue, which is our favourite colour. It is extracted from a berry, and is brighter and richer than any I have seen in Europe. Besides this, our women of distinction wear golden ornaments, which they dispose with some profusion on their arms and legs. When our women are not employed with the men in tillage, their usual occupation is spinning and weaving cotton, which they after-wards dye, and make into garments. They also manufacture earthen vessels, of which we have many kinds. Among the rest tobacco pipes, made after the same fashion, and used in the same manner, as those in Turkey.

Our manner of living is entirely plain; for as yet the natives are unacquainted with those refinements in cookery which debauch the taste: bullocks, goats, and poultry, supply the greatest part of their food. These constitute likewise the principal wealth of the country, and the chief articles of its commerce. The flesh is usually stewed in a pan.

Making palm-wine in a Nigerian village, a nineteenth-century lithograph.

To make it savoury we sometimes use also pepper and other spices; and we have salt made of wood ashes. Our vegetables are mostly plantains, eadas, yams, beans, and Indian corn. The head of the family usually eats alone; his wives and slaves have also their separate tables. Before we taste food, we always wash our hands; indeed our cleanliness on all occasions is extreme; but on this it is an indispensable ceremony. After washing, libation is made, by pouring out a small portion of the drink on the floor, and tossing a small quantity of the food in a certain place, for the spirits of departed relations, which the natives suppose to preside over their conduct, and guard them from evil. They are totally unacquainted with strong or spirituous liquors; and their principal beverage is palm wine. This is got from a tree of that name, by tapping it at the top, and fastening a large gourd to it; and sometimes one tree will yield three or four gallons in a night. When just drawn, it is of a most delicious sweetness, but in a few days it acquires a tartish and more spirituous flavour: though I never saw any one intoxicated by it. The same tree also produces nuts and oil. Our principal luxury is in perfumes; one sort of these is an odoriferous wood of delicious fragrance: the other a kind of earth; a small portion of which thrown into the fire diffuses a most powerful odour. We beat this wood into powder, and mix it with palm oil; with which both men and women perfume themselves.

31

In our buildings we study convenience rather than ornament. Each master of a family has a large square piece of ground, surrounded with a moat or fence, or inclosed with a wall made of red earth tempered, which, when dry is as hard as brick. Within this are his houses to accommodate his family and slaves; which, if numerous, frequently present the appearance of a village. In the middle stands the principal building, appropriated to the sole use of the master, and consisting of two apartments; in one of which he sits in the day with his family, the other is left apart for the reception of his friends. He has besides these a distinct apartment, in which he sleeps, together with his male children. On each side are the apartments of his wives, who have also their separate day and night houses. The habitations of the slaves and their families are distributed throughout the rest of the inclosure. . . .

As we live in a country where nature is prodigal of her favours, our wants are few, and easily supplied; of course we have few manufactures. They consist for the most part of calicoes, earthen ware, ornaments, and instruments of war and husbandry. But these make no part of our commerce, the principal articles of which, as I have observed, are provisions. In such a state money is of little use; however we have some small pieces of coin, if I may call them such. . . . We have also markets, at which I have been frequently with my mother. These are sometimes visited by stout mahogany-coloured men from the southwest of us: we call them *Oye-Eboe*, which term signifies red men living at a distance. They generally bring us fire-arms, gunpowder, hats, beads, and dried fish. The last we esteemed a great rarity, as our waters were only brooks and springs. These articles they barter with us for odoriferous woods and earth, and our salt of wood-ashes. They always carry slaves through our land; but the strictest account is exacted of their manner of procuring them before they are suffered to pass. Sometimes indeed we sold slaves to them, but they were only prisoners of war, or such among us as had been convicted of kidnapping, or adultery, and some other crimes, which we esteemed heinous. This practice of kidnapping induces me to think, that, notwithstanding all our strictness, their principal business among us was to trepan our people. I remember too they carried great sacks along with them, which not long after I had an opportunity of fatally seeing applied to that infamous purpose.

Our land is uncommonly rich and fruitful, and produces all kinds of vegetables in great abundance. We have plenty of Indian corn, and vast quantities of cotton and tobacco. Our pine apples grow without culture; they are about the size of the largest sugar-loaf and finely flavoured. We have also spices of different kinds, particularly pepper; and a variety of delicious fruits which I have never seen in Europe; together with gums of various kinds, and honey in abundance. All our industry

Street of the guild of the bronze and brass casters of Benin.

33

is exerted to improve those blessings of nature. Agriculture is our chief employment; and every one, even the children and women, are engaged in it. Thus we are all habituated to labour from our earliest years. Every one contributes something to the common stock; and, as we are unacquainted with idleness, we have no beggars. The benefits of such a mode of living are obvious. The West India planters prefer the slaves of Benin or Eboe to those of any other part of Guinea, for their hardiness, intelligence, integrity, and zeal. Those benefits are felt by us in the general healthiness of the people, and in their vigour and activity; I might have added too in their comeliness. Deformity is indeed unknown amongst us, I mean that of shape. Numbers of the natives of Eboe, now in London, might be brought in support of this assertion; for, in regard to complexion, ideas of beauty are wholly relative. I remember while in Africa to have seen three negro children, who were tawny, and another quite white, who were universally regarded by myself and the natives in general, as far as related to their complexions, as deformed. Our women too were, in my eyes at least, uncommonly graceful, alert, and modest to a degree of bashfulness; nor do I remember to have ever heard of an instance of incontinence amongst them before marriage. They are also remarkably cheerful. Indeed cheerfulness and affability are two of the leading characteristics of our nation.

. . . As to religion, the natives believe that there is one Creator of all things, and that he lives in the sun, and is girded round with a belt, that he may never eat or drink; but according to some, he smokes a pipe, which is our own favourite luxury. They believe he governs events, especially our deaths or captivity; but, as for the doctrine of eternity, I do not remember to have ever heard of it: some however believe in the transmigration of souls in a certain degree. Those spirits, which are not transmigrated, such as their dear friends or relations, they believe always attend them, and guard them from the bad spirits of their foes. For this reason, they always, before eating, as I have observed, put some small portion of the meat, and pour some of their drink, on the ground for them; and they often make oblations of the blood of beasts or fowls at their graves. I was very fond of my mother, and almost constantly with her. When she went to make these oblations at her mother's tomb, which was a kind of small solitary thatched house, I sometimes attended her. There she made her libations, and spent most of the night in cries and lamentations. I have often been extremely terrified on these occasions. The loneliness of the place, the darkness of the night, and the ceremony of libation, naturally awful and gloomy, were heightened by my mother's lamentations; and these concurring with the doleful cries of birds, by which these places were frequented, gave an inexpressible terror to the scene.

THE WRESTLERS

(Excerpt from Things Fall Apart*)*

Chinua Achebe

The whole village turned out on the *ilo*, men, women and children. They stood round in a huge circle leaving the centre of the playground free. The elders and grandees of the village sat on their own stools brought there by their young sons or slaves. Okonkwo was among them. All others stood except those who came early enough to secure places on the few stands which had been built by placing smooth logs on forked pillars.

The wrestlers were not there yet and the drummers held the field. They too sat just in front of the huge circle of spectators, facing the elders. Behind them was the big and ancient silk-cotton tree which was sacred. Spirits of good children lived in that tree waiting to be born. On ordinary days young women who desired children came to sit under its shade.

There were seven drums and they were arranged according to their sizes in a long wooden basket. Three men beat them with sticks, working feverishly from one drum to another. They were possessed by the spirit of the drums.

The young men who kept order on these occasions dashed about, consulting among themselves and with the leaders of the two wrestling teams, who were still outside the circle, behind the crowd. Once in a while two young men carrying palm fronds ran round the circle and kept the crowd back by beating the ground in front of them or, if they were stubborn, their legs and feet.

At last the two teams danced into the circle and the crowd roared and clapped. The drums rose to a frenzy. The people surged forward. The young men who kept order flew around, waving their palm fronds. Old men nodded to the beat of the drums and remembered the days when they wrestled to its intoxicating rhythm.

The contest began with boys of fifteen or sixteen. There were only three such boys in each team. They were not the real wrestlers; they merely set the scene. Within a short time the first two bouts were over. But the third created a big sensation even among the elders who did not usually show their excitement so openly. It was as quick as the other two, perhaps even quicker. But very few people had ever seen that kind of wrestling before. As soon as the two boys closed in, one of them did something which no one could describe because it had been as quick as a flash. And the other boy was flat on his back. The crowd roared and clapped and for a while drowned the frenzied drums. Okonkwo sprang to his feet and quickly sat down again. Three young men from the victorious boy's team ran forward, carried him shoulder-high and danced through the cheering crowd. Everybody soon knew who the boy was. His name was Maduka, the son of Obierika.

The drummers stopped for a brief rest before the real matches. Their bodies shone with sweat, and they took up fans and began to fan themselves. They also drank water from small pots and ate kola nuts. They became ordinary human beings again, talking and laughing among themselves and with others who stood near them. The air, which had been stretched taut with excitement, relaxed again. It was as if water had been poured on the tightened skin of a drum. Many people looked around, perhaps for the first time, and saw those who stood or sat next to them.

'I did not know it was you,' Ekwefi said to the woman who had stood shoulder to shoulder with her since the beginning of the matches.

'I do not blame you,' said the woman. 'I have never seen such a large crowd of people. Is it true that Okonkwo nearly killed you with his gun?'

'It is true indeed, my dear friend. I cannot yet find a mouth with which to tell the story.'

'Your *chi* is very much awake, my friend. And how is my daughter, Ezinma?'

'She has been very well for some time now. Perhaps she has come to stay.'

'I think she has. How old is she now?'

'She is about ten years old.'

'I think she will stay. They usually stay if they do not die before the age of six.'

'I pray she stays,' said Ekwefi with a heavy sigh.

The woman with whom she talked was called Chielo. She was the priestess of Agbala, the Oracle of the Hills and the Caves. In ordinary life Chielo was a widow with two children. She was very friendly with Ekwefi and they shared a common shed in the market. She was particularly fond of Ekwefi's only daughter, Ezinma, whom she called 'my daughter'. Quite often she bought bean-cakes and gave Ekwefi some to take home to Ezinma. Anyone seeing Chielo in ordinary life would hardly believe she was the same person who prophesied when the spirit of Agbala was upon her.

*

The drummers took up their sticks again and the air shivered and grew tense like a tightened bow.

The two teams were ranged facing each other across the clear space. A young man from one team danced across the centre to the other side

Door of a Yoruba palace representing everyday life and festivities.

and pointed at whomever he wanted to fight. They danced back to the centre together and then closed in.

There were twelve men on each side and the challenge went from one side to the other. Two judges walked around the wrestlers and when they thought they were equally matched, stopped them. Five matches ended in this way. But the really exciting moments were when a man was thrown. The huge voice of the crowd then rose to the sky and in every direction. It was even heard in the surrounding villages.

The last match was between the leaders of the teams. They were among the best wrestlers in all the nine villages. The crowd wondered who would throw the other this year. Some said Okafo was the better man; others said he was not the equal of Ikezue. Last year neither of them had thrown the other even though the judges had allowed the contest to go on longer than was the custom. They had the same style and one saw the other's plans beforehand. It might happen again this year.

Dusk was already approaching when their contest began. The drums went mad and the crowds also. They surged forward as the two young men danced into the circle. The palm fronds were helpless in keeping them back.

Ikezue held out his right hand. Okafo seized it, and they closed in. It was a fierce contest. Ikezue strove to dig in his right heel behind Okafo so as to pitch him backwards in the clever *ege* style. But the one knew what the other was thinking. The crowd had surrounded and swallowed up the drummers, whose frantic rhythm was no longer a mere disembodied sound but the very heart-beat of the people.

The wrestlers were now almost still in each other's grip. The muscles on their arms and their thighs and on their backs stood out and twitched. It looked like an equal match. The two judges were already moving forward to separate them when Ikezue, now desperate, went down quickly on one knee in an attempt to fling his man backwards over his head. It was a sad miscalculation. Quick as the lightning of Amadiora, Okafo raised his right leg and swung it over his rival's head. The crowd burst into a thunderous roar. Okafo was swept off his feet by his supporters and carried home shoulder-high. They sang his praise and the young women clapped their hands:

> 'Who will wrestle for our village?
>   Okafo will wrestle for our village.
> Has he thrown a hundred men?
>   He has thrown four hundred men.
> Has he thrown a hundred Cats?
>   He has thrown four hundred Cats.
> Then send him word to fight for us.'

AGBOR DANCER

John Pepper Clark

See her caught in the throb of a drum
Tippling from hide-brimmed stem
Down lineal veins to ancestral core,
Opening out in her supple tan limbs
Like fresh foliage in the sun.

See how entangled in the magic maze of music
In trance she treads the intricate pattern,
Rippling crest after crest to meet
The green clouds of the forest.

Tremulous beats wake trenchant
In heart a descant
Tingling quick to her finger tips
And toes virginal habits long
Too atrophied for pen or tongue.

Could I, early sequestered from my tribe,
Free a lead-tethered scribe,
I would answer her communal call,
Lose myself in her warm caress
Intervolving earth, sky and flesh.

BENIN AND NEIGHBOURHOOD

Mary Kingsley

According to Clapperton the Benin people are descendants of the Yoruba tribes, the Yoruba tribes being descended from six brothers, all the sons of one mother. Their names were Ikelu, Egba, Ijebu, Ifé, Ibini (Benin) and Yoruba.

According to the late Sultan Bello (the Foulah chief of Sokoto at the time of Captain Clapperton's visit to that city), the Yoruba tribes are descended from the children of Canaan, who were of the tribe of Nimrod.

In my opinion there is room for much speculation on this statement of the Sultan Bello.

It is a very curious fact that the people of Benin City have been, from the earliest accounts we have of them, great workers in brass. Might not the ancestors of this people have brought the art of working in brass with them from the far distant land of Canaan? Moses, when speaking of the land of Canaan, says, 'out of whose hills thou mayest dig brass' (Deut. 8:9). Here we must understand copper to be meant; because brass is not dug out of the earth, but copper is, and found in abundance in that part of the world.

Yet another curious subject for reflection, from the first information that European travellers give us (*circa* 1485) in their descriptions of the city of Benin, mention has invariably been made of towers, from the summits of which monster brass serpents were suspended. Upon the entry of the punitive expedition into Benin City in February, 1897, Benin City still possessed one of these serpents in brass, not hanging from a tower, but laid upon the roof of one of the king's houses.

Might not these brazen serpents be a remnant of some tradition handed down from the time of Moses? For do we not read in the Scriptures, that the people of Israel had sinned; and God to punish them sent fiery serpents, which bit the people, and many died. Then Moses cried to God, and God told him to make a serpent of brass, and set it on a pole (Numbers 21:9).

While on the subject of serpents, I may mention that in the neighbourhood of Benin, there is a *ju-ju* ordeal pond or river, said to be infested with dangerous and poisonous snakes and alligators, through which a man accused of any crime passing unscathed proves his innocence.

There are some other customs connected with the position of the king of Benin, as the head of the *ju-ju*-ism of his country, which seem to have some trace of a Biblical origin, but which I will not discuss here, but leave to the ethnologists to unravel, if they can.

Detail of bead work from dress of a magical figure in Yoruba woodcarving in Ibadan University Museum.

Esku is an essential figure in Yoruba households, to ensure success in communication with the spirits.

41

That they were a superior people to the surrounding tribes is amply demonstrated by their being workers in brass and iron; displaying considerable art in some of their castings in brass, iron, copper and bronze, their carving in ivory, and their manufacture of cotton cloth— no other people in the Delta showing any such ability.

The Jakri tribe, who inhabit that part of the country lying between the Sobo country and the Ijo country, were the dominant tribe in the lower or New Benin country. Being themselves tributary to the Benin king, they dare not make the Sobo or Ijo men pay a direct tribute to them for the right to live, but they indirectly took a much larger tribute from them than ever they paid to the king of Benin.

. . . The Jakri tribe claim to be of the same race as the people of Benin City and Kingdom. This I am inclined to dispute; I think they were a coast tribe like the Ijos. Tradition says that Wari was founded by people from Benin kingdom and for many years was tributary to the king of Benin, but in 1778 Wari was reported to be quite independent. They may have become almost the same race by intermarriage with the Benin people that went to Wari; but that they were originally the same race I say no.

The religion of the Jakri tribe and the native laws and system of ordeals were, as far as I have been able to ascertain, identical with those of the Benin kingdom; with the exception of the human sacrifices and their law of inheritance which does not admit the right of primogeniture —following in this respect, the laws of the Bonny men and their neighbours. Twin children are usually killed by the Jakris, and the mother driven into the bush to die.

The Jakri tribe are, without doubt, one of the finest in the Niger Coast Protectorate; many of their present chiefs are very honest and intelligent men, also excellent traders. Their women are noted as being the finest and best looking for miles round.

The Jakri women have already made great strides towards their complete emancipation from the low state in which the women of neighbouring tribes still find themselves, many of them being very rich and great traders.

The Sobo tribe have been kept so much in the background by the Jakris that little is known about them. What little is known of them is to their credit.

We now come to the Ijo tribe, or at least, that portion of them that live within the Niger Coast Protectorate; these men are reported by some travellers to be cannibals, and a very turbulent people; this character has been given them by interested parties. Their looks are very much against them as they disfigure their faces by heavy cuts as tribal marks, and some pick up the flesh between their eyes making a kind of ridge, that gives them a savage expression. Though I have put

A map of part of the Rivers Niger and Chadda surveyed and drawn by Commander W. Allen.

42

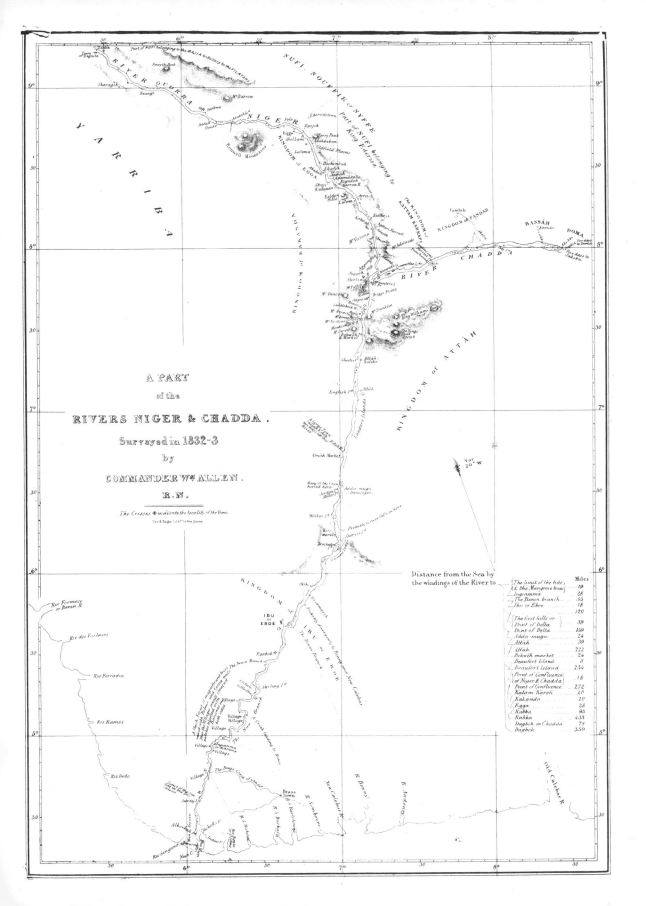

A PART
of the
RIVERS NIGER & CHADDA.
Surveyed in 1832-3
by
COMMANDER W.ᵐ ALLEN.
R.N.

The Crosses ✚ indicate the locality of the Views

Day & Haghe Lith.ˢ to the Queen

Distance from the Sea by the windings of the River to	Miles
The limit of the tide	19
& the Mangrove trees	
Ingramma	28
The Benin branch	55
Ibu or Eboe	18
	120
The first hills or Point of Delta	39
Point of Delta	150
Adda-muegu	24
Attàh	39
Attàh	222
Bokwèh market	24
Beaufort Island	8
Beaufort Island	254
Point of Confluence of Niger & Chadda	18
Point of Confluence	272
Kutam karah	20
Kakanda	20
Egga	28
Kabba	93
Rabba	433
Dagboh on Chadda	78
Dagboh	350

the limit of these people at the river Ramos, they really extend along the coast as far as the western bank of the Akassa River. They have never had a chance and, with the exception of large timber for making canoes, their country does not produce much. Though I have seen considerable numbers of rubber-producing trees in their country, I never was able to induce them to work it. No doubt they asked the advice of their *ju-ju* as to taking my advice, and he followed the usual rule laid down by the priesthood of *ju-ju*-ism, no innovations.

Whilst I was in the Ijo country I carefully studied their *ju-ju*, as I had been told they were great believers in, and practisers of *ju-ju*-ism. I found little in their system differing from that practised in most of the rivers of the Delta.

In all these practices human agency plays a very large part, and this seems to be known even to the lower orders of the people; as an instance, I must here relate an experience I once had amongst the Ijos. I had arranged with a chief living on the Bassa Creek to lend me his fastest canoe and twenty-five of his people, to take me to the Brass River; the bargain was that his canoe should be ready at Cock-Crow Peak the following morning. I was ready at the water-side by the time appointed, but only about six of the smallest boys had put in an appearance; the old chief was there in a most furious rage, sending off messengers in all directions to find the canoe boys. After about two hours' work and the expenditure of much bad language on the part of the old chief, also some hard knocks administered to the canoe boys by the men who had been sent after them, as evidenced by the wales I saw on their backs, the canoe was at last manned, and I took my seat in it under a very good mat awning which nearly covered the canoe from end to end, and thanking my stars that now my troubles had come to an end I hoped at least for a time. I was, however, a very big bit too premature, for before the old chief would let the canoe start, he informed me he must make *ju-ju* for the safety of his canoe and the safe return of it and all his boys, to say nothing of my individual safety.

One of the first requirements of that particular *ju-ju* cost me further delay, for a bottle of gin had to be procured, and as the daily market in that town had not yet opened, and no public house had yet been established by any enterprising Ijo, it took some time to procure.

On the arrival of the article, however, my friend the old chief proceeded in a most impressive manner to repeat a short prayer, the principal portion I was able to understand and which was as follows: 'I beg you, I beg you, don't capsize my canoe. If you do, don't drown any of my boys and don't do any harm to my friend the white man.' This was addressed to the spirit of the water; having finished this little prayer, he next sprinkled a little gin about the bows of the canoe and in the river, afterwards taking a drink himself. He then produced a leaf

with about an ounce of broken-up cooked yam mixed with a little palm oil, which he carefully fixed in the extreme foremost point of the canoe.

At last this ceremony was at an end and we started off, but alas! my troubles were only just beginning. We had been started about half an hour, and I had quietly dozed off into a pleasant sleep, when I was awakened by feeling the canoe rolling from side to side as if we were in rough water; just then the boys all stopped pulling, and on my remonstrance they informed me *ju-ju* 'no will', *id est*, that the *ju-ju* had told them they must go back. I used gentle persuasion in the form of offers of extra pay at first, then I stormed and used strong language, or at least, what little Ijo strong language I knew, but all to no avail. I then began to inquire what *ju-ju* had spoken, and they pointed out a small bird that just then flew away into the bush; it looked to me something like a kingfisher. The head boy of the canoe then explained to me that this *ju-ju* bird having spoken, *id est*, chirped on the right-hand side of the canoe, and the goat's skull hanging up to the foremost awning stanchion having fallen the same way (this ornament I had not previously noticed), signified that we must turn back. So turn back we did, though I thought at the time the boys did not want to go the journey, owing to the almost continual state of quarrelling that had been going on for years between the Ijos and the Brassmen. I was not far wrong, for when we eventually did arrive at Brass, I had to hide these Ijo people in the hold of my ship, as the very sight of a Brassman made them shiver.

The following morning the same performance was gone through; we started, and at about the same point *ju-ju* spoke again; again we returned. My old friend the chief was very sorry he said, but he could not blame his boys for acting as they had done, *ju-ju* having told them to return. He would not listen when I told him I felt confident his boys had assisted the *ju-ju* by making the canoe roll about from side to side.

However, I thought the matter over to myself during that second day, and decided I would make sure one part of that *ju-ju* should not speak against me the next morning, and that was the goat's skull, so during that night after every Ijo was fast asleep, I visited that skull and carefully secured it to its post by a few turns of very fine fishing line in such a manner that no one could notice what I had done, if they did not specially examine it. I dare not fix it to the left, that being the favourable side, for fear of it being noticed, but I fixed it straight up and down, so that it could not demonstrate against my journey.

I retired to my sleeping quarters and slept the sleep of the just, and next morning started in the best of spirits, though continually haunted by the fear that my little strategem might be discovered. We had got about the same distance from the town that we had on the two previous mornings when the canoe began to oscillate as usual, caused by a combined movement of all the boys in the canoe, I was perfectly con-

A Scene on the River Niger, from Commander Allen's sketchbooks.

vinced, for the creek we were in was as smooth as a mill pond. Many anxious glances were cast at the skull, and the canoe was made to roll more and more until the water slopped over into her, but the skull did not budge, and, strange to relate, the bird of ill omen did not show itself or chirp this morning, so the boys gave up making the canoe oscillate and commenced to paddle for all they were worth, and the following evening we arrived at my ship in Brass. We could have arrived much earlier, but the Ijos did not wish to meet with any Brassmen, so we waited until the shades of night came on, and thus passed unobserved several Brass canoes, arriving safely at my ship in time for dinner.

I carefully questioned the head boy of the Ijo boys all about this bird that had given me so much trouble. He explained to me that once having passed a certain point in the creek, the bird not having spoken and the skull not having demonstrated either, it was quite safe to continue on our journey, conveying to me the idea that this bird was a regular inhabitant of a certain portion of the bush, which was also their sacred bush wherein the *ju-ju* priests practised their most private devotions. The same species of bird showed itself several times both on the right of us and on the left of us as we passed through other creeks on our way to Brass, but the canoe boys took no notice of it.

PIANO AND DRUMS

Gabriel Okara

When at break of day at a riverside
I hear jungle drums telegraphing
the mystic rhythm, urgent, raw
like bleeding flesh, speaking of
primal youth and the beginning,
I see the panther ready to pounce,
the leopard snarling about to leap
and the hunters crouch with spears poised;

And my blood ripples, turns torrent,
topples the years and at once I'm
in my mother's lap a suckling;
at once I'm walking simple
paths with no innovations,
rugged, fashioned with the naked
warmth of hurrying feet and groping hearts
in green leaves and wild flowers pulsing.

Then I hear a wailing piano
solo speaking of complex ways
in tear-furrowed concerto;
of faraway lands
and new horizons with
coaxing diminuendo, counterpoint,
crescendo. But lost in the labyrinth
of its complexities, it ends in the middle
of a phrase at a daggerpoint.

And I, lost in the morning mist
of an age at a riverside, keep
wandering in the mystic rhythm
of jungle drums and the concerto.

*Benin ivory leopard decorated
with bronze studs.*

47

HOW LAGOS BECAME A COLONY

Sir Richard Burton

Evening placed us in the roads of Lagos. A mild evening: the wind was hushed, and the heat oppressive. It is said to average 10°F hotter at this place than in Lagos town. Against the purple-black surface of the eastern sky the bar was smoking forth a white vapour, as if afraid to break, and we could hear from afar the muffled roar of the sullen surf. We and our fellow-sufferers, six or seven merchantmen, lay broadside on, with a monotonous ceaseless roll, which seems to drive comfort out of a ship. Many must pass months in this most unpleasant sing-swong till they have taken in cargo. We are lying in the French roads, four miles eastward of the entrance or English roads. As night was near, not a canoe would put off from the shore. I spent my *soirée* in the study of bars. The bar is a notable formation in Western, as in Eastern Africa. . . .

The favourite seat of a bar is at the mouth of a river or an outfall which is liable to be much swollen by the rains. From the inland comes a mass of matter mechanically suspended, and sometimes floating islets, which will trip vessels from their anchors; when the emission meets the tide, deposition takes place, and goes on increasing. Some bars are therefore of mud; others, where the sea has greater power, are sand hard as stone. The heaviness of the ocean swell is attributed by certain writers to distant storms; others, especially Captain Fishbourne, to a 'want of hydrostatic equilibrium'.

No one seems to visit Lagos for the first time without planning a breakwater. About three years ago an American company proposed to make floating breakwaters, upon the condition of receiving the harbour dues for twenty years; Jonathan, however, was refused.

The site of the town, four miles from the entrance, is detestable; unfortunately, there is no better within many a league. It occupies the western side of an islet about three miles and a half long from north-east to south-west, by one broad from north to south; it is formed by two offsets from the Ikoradu (Cradoo) coast, namely, the Ossa River, opposite, and Five Cowrie Creek behind the settlement.

The first aspect is as if a hole had been hollowed out in the original mangrove forest that skirts the waters, where bush and dense jungle, garnished with many a spreading tree, tall palms, and matted mass of fetid verdure rise in terrible profusion around. The soil is sandy, and in parts there are depressions which the rains convert into black and muddy ponds; the ground, however, is somewhat higher in the interior, where the race-course lies. The gap of the Ossa or Badagry Lagoon, is

The Harbour of Lagos.
(Photo Dr Georg Gerster)

nearly opposite the town; and on the other side there is low, swampy ground, a clay formation, which retains the water, and which adds something more to the evils of the place. The thin line of European buildings that occupy the best sites, fronting the water, are, first, the French *comptoir*, prettily surrounded with gardens; then a large pretentious building, white and light yellow, lately raised by M. Carrena, a Sardinian merchant—it is said to be already decaying; then the Wesleyan mission-house; the Hamburghers' factory; the Wesleyan chapel, with about five times its fair amount of ground; the British consulate, like that at Fernando Po, a corrugated iron coffin or plank-lined morgue, containing a dead consul once a year; the Church mission-house, whose overgrown compound caused such pretty squabbles in days gone by, and which, between whiles, served as a church; another Sardinian factory; a tall whitewashed and slated house, built by Mr McCoskry; and at the furthest end, another establishment of Hamburghers, who at present have more than their share of the local commerce: these are the only salient points of the scene. They are interspersed with tenements of less pretensions, 'suam quisque domum spatio circumdat', a custom derived by the Anglo-Indians through the England and the Germany of Tacitus's day; and the thin line is backed by a large native town, imperceptible from the sea, and mainly fronting the Ikoradu Lake. . . .

The afternoon was devoted to inspecting the town, which is native to the last degree. It is said to be five miles in circumference, and containing 30,000 inhabitants, of whom 700 to 800 are Moslems. Like the people of Badagry and Porto Novo, the Lagosans are of Popo race, and many of them are originally Beninese. The eastern is here the 'west end', and there have been the usual quarrels for frontage, each factory and mission-house wishing to secure for itself as much, and to leave its neighbour as little, as possible. The native town, which is divided into sundry quarters, Okofája, Obebowo, Offí, and Eggá, which contains the palace of the now destitute Docemo, is to the west of the 'Garden Reach', and stretches over the interior of the island. The streets want only straightening, widening, draining, and cleaning. . . . Like Jericho, it is a city of palms: the cocoa grows almost in the salt water; the broad-leaved bread-fruit, introduced from the far Polynesian lands, has taken root like an indigen; and in the branches of the papaw nestle amadavats, orioles, and brilliant palm-birds.

Lagos is a young and thriving place. Its position points it out as the natural key of this part of Africa, and the future emporium of all Yoruba, between the Niger and the sea. It cannot help commanding commerce: even under the wretched management of the native princes, it attracted the whole trade of the Benin country. In proper hands it will be the sole outlet of trade from Central Guinea and the Sudan,

50

lands teeming with various wealth—palm oil, cotton, shea-butter, metals, native cloths, sugar, indigo, tobacco of good quality, and ivory; in the neighbourhood of Ilorin, about eight days' journey north of Abeokuta, it is not worth their while, on account of the heavy tolls, to export their tusks. At present the bar is an obstacle to improvement; time, however, will remedy that. The roads require attention, but they are hardly so important to Africa as people at home suppose. In these prairie lands a path is easily cut, and soon becomes a rut impracticable to an Englishman or a horse, but perfectly fitted for the African. Were you to give him the finest highway in Europe, after a year he would have worn a deep track by marching in Indian file, and the rest would be a bright expanse of verdure. . . .

The town of Lagos is certainly one of the most unhealthy spots on these malarious shores, but the climate may be mitigated. As the people do not bury in their ground-floors, it is here easy to remove a house. Broad streets, admitting free currents of air, and perfectly drained, should run the whole length of the settlement parallel with the Lagoon, and at right angles to these, cross ways from the water side to the interior would supply ample ventilation. The site has a good slope towards the flowing stream which is a ready-made *cloaca maxima*, and very little cutting would draw off the rains, which now stand long upon the stiff hardened sand.

. . . I am certain that Lagos, when ten years old, will be able to provide for itself, and that in ten more it would become the emporium of the great and rich Yoruba and Dahomian countries, whose natural adit and issue it is.

. . . Lagos was born in the British family, the youngest member of her colonies, on the 6th day of August, AD 1861. Commander Bedingfield, R.N., after a hard bumping on the bar off the east spit, had by high direction entered into a palaver with Docemo, king of Lagos, and after 'jamming heads' . . . informed him that permanent occupation (a nicer word than annexation) was determined upon, and that he, Docemo, was to be pensioned, and become one of the many kings lately 'retired from business'. That barbarous person, curious to say, was not delighted by the intelligence. In fact, he made some difficulties. He proposed to meet Her Majesty's consul, 'the Captain', and all the British merchants at Palma, a French station some thirty miles east of Lagos, where he probably intended to give them something more than a bit of his mind. They politely declined a trip so far out of the range of the Promethean fire.

So matters ran till the 5th of August, when a flagstaff was slipped and rigged near the British consulate, and Commander Bedingfield landed with his marines.

KANO'S SLAVE MARKET 1825

Hugh Clapperton

A slave trader selecting slaves in a market; from an old engraving.

The slave market is held in two long sheds, one for males, the other for females, where they are seated in rows, and carefully decked out for the exhibition; the owner, or one of his trusty slaves, sitting near them. Young or old, plump or withered, beautiful or ugly, are sold without distinction; but, in other respects, the buyer inspects them with the utmost attention, and somewhat in the same manner as a volunteer seaman is examined by a surgeon on entering the navy: he looks at the tongue, teeth, eyes, and limbs, and endeavours to detect rupture by a forced cough. If they are afterwards found to be faulty or unsound, or even without any specific objection, they may be returned within three days. When taken home, they are stripped of their finery, which is sent back to their former owner. Slavery is here so common, or the mind of slaves is so constituted, that they always appeared much happier than their masters; the women, especially, singing with the greatest glee all the time they are at work. People become slaves by birth or by capture in war. The Felatahs frequently manumit slaves at the death of their master, or on the occasion of some religious festival. The letter of manumission must be signed before the cadi, and attested by two witnesses; and the mark of a cross is used by the illiterate among them, just as with us. The male slaves are employed in the various trades of building, working in iron, weaving, making shoes or clothes, and in traffic; the female slaves in spinning, baking, and selling water in the streets. Of the various people who frequent Kano, the *Nyffuans* are most celebrated for their industry; as soon as they arrive, they go to market and buy cotton for their women to spin, who, if not employed in this way, make *billam* for sale, which is a kind of flummery made of flour and tamarinds. The very slaves of this people are in great request, being invariably excellent tradesmen; and when once obtained, are never sold again out of the country.

Kano market today, a mobile locksmith's shop. (Photo George Rodger, MAGNUM)

52

KING OBI'S PALAVER

W. Allen and T. R. H. Thomson

Obi Osaï was attended by his judge, or 'King's-mouth', Amorama, and several of the *magnates of the land*, together with some of his brothers and children. He was dressed in a serjeant-major's coat, given him by Lander, and a loose pair of scarlet trousers presented to him on the same occasion. A conical black velvet cap was stuck on his head in a slanting manner. He brought a present of two small buffaloes and 250 yams; a very acceptable accompaniment.

On being shown to the after-part of the quarterdeck, where seats were provided for himself and the commissioners, he sat down to collect his scattered ideas, which appeared to be somewhat bewildered; and after a few complimentary remarks from Captain Trotter and the other commissioners, the conference was opened.

Captain Trotter, Senior Commissioner, explained to Obi Osaï, that Her Majesty the Queen of Great Britain had sent him and the three other gentlemen composing the Commission, to endeavour to enter into treaties with African chiefs for the abolition of the trade in human beings, which Her Majesty and all the British nation held to be an injustice to their fellow-creatures, and repugnant to the laws of God; that the vessels which he saw were not trading ships, but belonging to our queen, and were sent, at great expense, expressly to convey the commissioners appointed by Her Majesty, for the purpose of carrying out her benevolent intentions, for the benefit of Africa. Captain Trotter therefore requested the king to give a patient hearing to what the commissioners had to say to him on the subject.

Obi expressed himself through his interpreter, or 'mouth', much gratified at our visit; that he understood what was said, and would pay attention.

The commissioners then explained that the principal object in inviting him to a conference was, to point out the injurious effects to himself and to his people of the practice of selling their slaves, thus depriving themselves of their services for ever, for a trifling sum; whereas, if these slaves were kept at home, and employed in the cultivation of the land, in collecting palm oil, or other productions of the country for commerce, they would prove a permanent source of revenue. Obi replied, that he was very willing to do away with the slave-trade, if a better traffic could be substituted. With a view to elicit information, as well as more fully to explain our object, a number of queries were put to the king, some of which are given below, in order to illustrate the nature of our conference. . . .

Commissioners Does Obi sell slaves for his own dominions?

Obi No; they come from countries far away.

Commissioners Does Obi make war to procure slaves?

Obi When other chiefs quarrel with me and make war, I take all I can as slaves.

Commissioners What articles of trade are best suited to your people, or what would you like to be brought to your country?

Obi Cowries, cloth, muskets, powder, handkerchiefs, coral beads, hats —anything from the white man's country will please.

Commissioners You are the king of this country, as our queen is the sovereign of Great Britain; but she does not wish to trade with you; she only desires that her subjects may trade fairly with yours. Would they buy salt?

Obi Yes.

Commissioners The Queen of England's subjects would be glad to trade for raw cotton, indigo, ivory, gums, camwood. Now have your people these things to offer in return for English trade-goods?

Obi Yes.

Commissioners Englishmen will bring everything to trade but rum or spirits, which are injurious. If you induce your subjects to cultivate the ground, you will all become rich; but if you sell slaves, the land will not be cultivated, and you will become poorer by the traffic. If you do all these things which we advise you for your own benefit, our queen will grant you, for your own profit and revenue, one out of every twenty articles sold by British subjects in the Abòh territory; so that the more you persuade your people to exchange native produce for British goods, the richer you will become. You will then have a regular profit, enforced by treaty, instead of trusting to a 'dash' or present, which depends on the willingness of the traders.

Obi I will agree to discontinue the slave-trade, but I expect the English to bring goods for traffic.

Commissioners The queen's subjects cannot come here to trade, unless they are certain of a proper supply of your produce.

Obi I have plenty of palm oil.

Commissioners Mr Schön, a missionary, will explain to you in the Ibu language what the queen wishes; and if you do not understand, it shall be repeated.

Mr Schön began to read the address drawn up for the purpose of showing the different tribes what the views of the expedition were; but Obi soon appeared to be tired of a palaver which lasted so much longer than those to which he was accustomed. He manifested some impatience, and at last said: 'I have made you a promise to drop this slave-trade, and do not wish to hear anything more about it.'

Commissioners Our queen will be much pleased if you do, and you will receive the presents which she sent for you. When people in the white man's country sign a treaty or agreement, they always abide by it. The queen cannot come to speak to you, Obi Osaï, but she sends us to make the treaty for her.

Obi I can only engage my word for my own country.

Commissioners You cannot sell your slaves if you wish, for our queen has many warships at the mouth of the river, and Spaniards are afraid to come and buy there.

Obi I understand.

Commissioners Wicked white men come and buy slaves; not to eat them as your people believe, but to make them work harder than they can bear, by flogging and ill-using them. The English queen wishes to prevent such cruelty.

Obi I believe everything you have said, and I once more consent to give up the slave-trade.

Commissioners We wish to know if you are willing to stop boats carrying slaves through the waters of your dominions?

Obi Yes, very willing; except those I do not see.

Commissioners Also to prevent slaves being carried over your land?

Obi Certainly; but the English must furnish me and my people with arms, as my doing so will involve me in war with my neighbours.

Obi then retired for a short time to consult with his headmen.

Commissioners—*(on his return)*—Have you power to make an agreement with the commissioners in the name of all your subjects?

Obi I am the king. What I say is law. Are there two kings in England? There is only one here.

Commissioners Understanding you have sovereign power, can you seize slaves on the river?

Obi Yes.

Commissioners You must set them free.

Obi Yes *(snapping his fingers several times)*.

Commissioners The boats must be destroyed.

Obi I will break the canoe, but kill no one.

Commissioners Suppose a man-of-war takes a canoe, and it is proved to be a slaver, the officer's word must be taken by the king. You, Obi, or some one for you, can be present to see justice done.

Obi I understand.

Commissioners Any new men coming henceforth to Abòh are not to be made slaves.

Obi Very good.

Commissioners If the queen makes a treaty with Obi, will his successors, on his death, abide by the same?

Obi They will do as I command. I want this palaver to be settled. I am tired of so much talking, and wish to go on shore.

Yoruba palace door representing the arrival of the British Commissioner.

TWO STRANGE WORLDS

Francesca Yetunde Pereira

Women,
What fools we are,
Invading unprotected
The world of men so alien,
And ever manifesting
Weakness in tenderness.

In that world of reason,
Is it not reason to give?
Willing converts
Ardent learners
Giving, giving.

But, fools—
Our hearts have lost
The room for reason.
Can we unlearn
That which was taught?

Can we survive?
How can we live?
The flame is out,
The cinders
Painful memories.

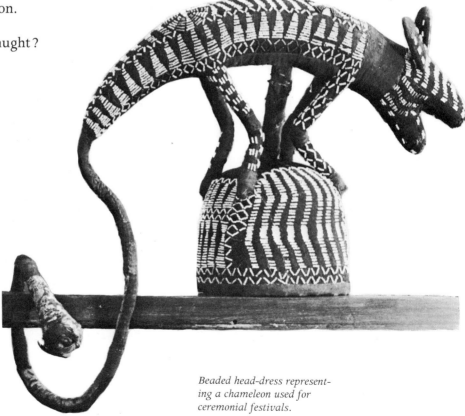

Beaded head-dress representing a chameleon used for ceremonial festivals.

58

HIGH LIFE FOR LIZARDS

(Excerpt)

Onuora Nzekwu

The dream was Ozoma, a tiny village in Onitsha. The time was late evening in November 1912, and Agom was tying on a brand-new wrapper that extended from her navel to just below her knees.

Concentric indigo-dye circles, cleverly drawn in free-hand round her navel, showed above the wrapper. They sent out a pair of long antennae which opened out until they found her precocious breasts and hugged the nipples in tight-fitting loops. Then they closed in again and met at the dagger point of her neckline before wandering off to caress her arms and back.

Rows of tight-fitting strings of cowrie shells sat high on her neck, apparently supporting her head. Her wide mouth, broad nose and two liquid, brown eyes were framed in an oval face topped by a crown of carefully plaited hair adorned with ivory pins and combs.

Shiny brass leglets rose in coils from her ankles to meet her cloth.

She put on her ivory bracelets and looked at herself in a mirror surrounded by a wooden frame with a handle. Then she turned and faced the two other girls in the room, who surveyed her critically. At last they nodded their satisfaction and followed her out of the room.

She was going to take leave of her relatives.

Halfway through the farewell greetings Agom turned and hurried away, as fast as her leglets could permit her, sobbing. She had longed for this very moment, but now when it came she could not stand it. Moments later she crossed the threshold of her home and stood gaping at the crowd that had gathered to honour her. A smile of gratitude softened her features—and she was lovely.

Soon after, the bridal procession formed. It was a grand procession and sang lustily as it wound its way through a couple of other Onitsha villages into a third, Ojele. Here were performed the final ceremonies which ended with the tying of the nuptial knot. Then members of the procession began to leave. Each wished Agom a happy home, lots of fun and an army of children before bidding her good night. One after another the lamps gave up their lights and darkness enveloped the village.

Agom's husband had exhausted himself trying to prove she knew no man before him. Now he lay beside her snoring off his tiredness; yet sleep would not cross Agom's eyes. The thought that it would soon be morning made her shut her eyes and refuse to think any more. But the moment her eyelids met, a cockerel flapped its wings somewhere

outside and crew. Its harsh voice jarred on her nerves and a cold shiver ran down her spine. She lay quietly waiting; waiting for the creaking and banging of doors, the pounding of strong feet running, urgent questions shot by anxious voices at no one in particular, the hurried flapping of wings, the squawking of a cockerel and then, silence—a silence which would be followed, moments later, by the less urgent creaking of doors as the men returned to their beds. She waited, but nothing happened, and she became uneasy.

It was taboo, in all the nine villages that made up the riverside town, for a cockerel to crow in the dead of night. Whenever the taboo was broken the offending cockerel met with instant death. For it was believed that its continued existence would alienate the affections of Ani, the earth goddess. Why then should Ojele allow this cockerel to live?

It was particularly annoying that the cockerel had chosen this very night, her home-coming night, to break the taboo. To every Onitsha woman her home-coming night was the most sacred in her life. It was the night she made her greatest sacrifice—her own blood—on the altar of her matrimonial home to gain her heart's most cherished desire—children.

The village was eerily quiet. Her husband lying beside her might well have been a log. She began to wonder what had come over the men of the village. Was there not one man enough to sacrifice the offending creature to ani and save her the ignominy of a desecrated home-coming night? As if in answer, an owl hooted mournfully somewhere out in the night. Then she heard footsteps outside their window, and, from the distance, the faint clucking of a cobra seeking to lure the stray, unwary hen to its death. Agom's head seemed to grow to twice its size.

In all her years in her father's house she had been brought up to regard these happenings as ill-omens. Her heart told her they added up to no good. Evil lurked somewhere; but where? Afraid, she nudged her husband into wakefulness. He put his strong arms round her and held her against him to reassure her.

Burial monuments showing Christian influence in a magician's compound in the Calabar tropical forest.

Ivory trumpet made by seventeenth-century Nigerian artists for the Portuguese Court.

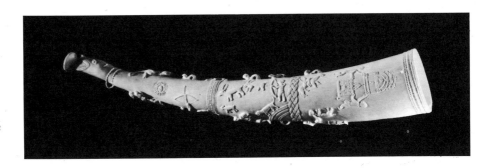

61

MY FATHER'S SLAVES

(Excerpt from Baba of Karo *by Mary Smith)*

Baba of Karo

This is how the slaves worked: each slave had his own farming land, if he had a wife she helped him, if he had none he worked alone, and if he had children they helped him too. In the early morning the slaves and their sons would go to their own farms. At this time of day (9.30 a.m.) they came back and went to the master's farm, the *gandu* fields, until Azahar (2.30) when they returned. At noon food was taken out to them at the *gandu* farm. At Azahar they came in and rested, then in the afternoon the men slaves went to their own farm-plots, and their wives and children went to their little plots too. Everyone grew guineacorn, cotton, millet, cowpeas, sweet potatoes, pumpkins, groundnuts, peppers, bitter tomatoes, sugar-cane, rice, *iburu*, okras, tomatoes and green peppers.

In the morning the slaves ate in their own compounds. At midday porridge made from the *gandu* grain was taken out to the slaves on the farm, while their wives ate grain from their own store at home. In the evening they all came to the front of our house and ate the *gandu* food of the master's house, each one took his own and they ate it there in front of our compound. The grain was divided out amongst the slaves' wives and they would grind it and bring back the flour to our compound and make the porridge. Everyone ate it, men and women and children—they did no cooking in their own homes except in the early morning. At midday and in the evening they all ate the *gandu* porridge. In the morning the master's head wife distributed grain to them and the slaves' wives ground the flour for the midday meal; then after that was eaten she gave them more grain and they ground the flour for the evening meal. It was cooked in a giant pot in our compound.

Whatever the slaves grew on their own farm-plots was their own, they took it to market to sell and bought gowns; their wives bought cloth and made ceremonial exchange-gifts. The slaves did not give their master any of their own farm produce, they did his work for him and that was that. If we had a ceremony, they all brought things to give us; if they had one we all took things to them, we took part in each other's ceremonies. When I was married they collected a bag of rice and a bag of grain, they packed the bags tight and gave them to the master as reinforcements. If the master's wife had a child, the slaves ground flour and made porridge and millet-balls, they killed a chicken and brought gifts on the naming day. They would all come to our entrance-hut on the naming day and eat.

Nigerian village scene in ne nineteenth century.

In the afternoons after work on the *gandu* farm was finished, some of the slaves worked at crafts. Some wove on the men's narrow loom, some were brokers in the market, some were salt-sellers, some sold kolanuts or sugar-cane or sweet potatoes or cotton, or other things. Some were dyers, some grew onions or sugar-cane in marsh-plots. Some just farmed their own plots. Those who did crafts had been born in the *rinji*; slaves who were bought in the market could not do anything except farming. If a slave had a son he would see a craftsman working, he would go and watch him and he would learn. The bought slaves spoke 'Gwari', but their children spoke Hausa.

Our slaves were from many tribes, there was no sort of slave that we hadn't got in our *rinji*. When they had children, the children were given our inherited facial marks, the Bare-bare mark down their nose. Not all masters gave their slaves' children their own marks. When the boys were seven years old they were taught to say their prayers and they went to the Koran school and learnt to recite passages from the Koran; some of the girls went, too. There were several teachers, Malam Yusufu and Malam Tanko and Malam Audu Bawan Allah. There was no *bori*-dancing in our hamlet except for one of our slaves, Mada, a Gwari, who was sometimes possessed. We used to go to the compounds of the prostitutes in Zarewa town and watch them *bori*-dancing.

Slaves sometimes escaped, our Tagwayi escaped and so did Hasada. Hasada ran away one night. You would hunt and hunt for them, and then one day you would hear that someone had seen them in a far-away town. If anyone questioned him the slave would say he had been sent to do an errand for his master. You never caught them again.

I remember when a European came to Karo on a horse, and some of his foot soldiers went into the town. Everyone came out to look at them, but in Zarewa they didn't see the European. Everyone at Karo ran away—'There's a European, there's a European!' He came from Zaria with a few black men, two on horses and four on foot. We were inside the town. Later on we heard that they were there in Zaria in crowds, clearing spaces and building houses. One of my younger 'sisters' was at Karo, she was pregnant, and when she saw the European she ran away and shut the door.

At that time Yusufu was the king of Kano. He did not like the Europeans, he did not wish them, he would not sign their treaty. Then he saw that perforce he would have to agree, so he did. We Habe wanted them to come, it was the Fulani who did not like it. When the Europeans came the Habe saw that if you worked for them they paid you for it, they didn't say, like the Fulani, 'Commoner, give me this! Commoner, bring me that!' Yes, the Habe wanted them; they saw no harm in them. From Zaria they came to Rogo, they were building their big road to Kano City. They called out the people and said they were to come and make the road, if there were trees in the way they cut them down. The Europeans paid them with goods, they collected the villagers together and each man brought his large hoe. Money was not much use to them, so the Europeans paid them with food and other things.

The Europeans said that there were to be no more slaves; if someone said 'Slave!' you could complain to the *alkali* who would punish the master who said it, the judge said 'That is what the Europeans have decreed'. The first order said that any slave, if he was younger than you, was your younger brother, if he was older than you he was your elder brother—they were all brothers of their master's family. No one used the word 'slave' any more. When slavery was stopped, nothing much happened at our *rinji* except that some slaves whom we had bought in the market ran away. Our own father went to his farm and worked, he and his son took up their large hoes; they loaned out their spare farms. Tsoho our father and Kadiri my brother with whom I live now and Babambo worked, they farmed guineacorn and millet and groundnuts and everything; before this they had supervised the slaves' work—now they did their own. When the midday food was ready, the women of the compound would give us children the food, one of us drew water, and off we went to the farm to take the men their food at the foot of a tree; I was about eight or nine at that time, I think.

LAMENT OF THE DRUMS

Christopher Okigbo

I

Lion-hearted cedar forest, gonads for our thunder,
Even if you are very far away, we invoke you:

Give us our hollow heads of long-drums . . .

Antelopes for the cedar forest, swifter messengers
Than flash-of-beacon-flame, we invoke you:

Hide us; deliver us from our nakedness . . .

Many-fingered canebrake, exile for our laughter,
Even if you are very far away, we invoke you:

Come: limber our raw hides of antelopes . . .

Thunder of tanks of giant iron steps of detonators,
Fail safe from the clearing, we implore you:

We are tuned for a feast-of-seven-souls . . .

II

And the drums once more
From our soot chamber,
From the cinerary tower
To the crowded clearing;

Long-drums, we awake
Like a shriek of incense,
The unheard sullen shriek
Of the funerary ram:

Liquid messengers of blood,
Like urgent telegrams,
We have never been deployed
For feast of antelopes . . .

*Top of a magic wand,
Yoruba.*

And to the Distant—but how shall we go?
The robbers will strip us of our tendons!

For we sense
With dog-nose a Babylonian capture,
The martyrdom
Blended into that chaliced vintage;

And savour
The incense and in high buskin,
Like a web
Of voices all rent by javelins.

But distant seven winds invite us and our cannons
To limber our membranes for a dance of elephants . . .

III

They are fishing today in the dark waters
Where the mariner is finishing his rest . . .

Palinurus, alone in a hot prison, you will keep
The dead sea awake with nightsong . . .

Silver of rivulets this side of the bridge,
Cascades of lily-livered laughter,
Fold-on-fold of raped, naked blue—
What memory has the sea of her lover?

Palinurus, unloved in your empty catacomb,
You will wear away through age alone . . .

Nothing remains, only smoke after storm—
Some strange Celaeno and her harpy crew,
Laden with night and their belly's excrement,
Profane all things with hooked feet and foul teeth—

Masks and beggar-masks without age or shadow:
Broken tin-gods whose vision is dissolved . . .

It is over, Palinurus, at least for you,
In your tarmac of night and fever-dew:

Ibo dance mask.

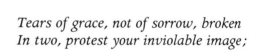

Tears of grace, not of sorrow, broken
In two, protest your inviolable image;

And the sultry waters, touched by the sun,
Inherit your paleness who reign, resigned

Like palm oil fostered in an ancient clay bowl;
A half-forgotten name: like a stifled sneeze . . .

Fishermen out there in the dark—O you
Who rake the waves or chase their wake—
Weave for him a shadow out of your laughter
For a dumb child to hide his nakedness . . .

IV

And the drums
Once more and like masked dancers,
On the orange—
Yellow myth of the sands of exile—

Long-drums dis-
Jointed, and with bleeding tendons,
Like tarantulas
Emptied of their bitterest poisons,

67

And to the Distant—but how shall we go?
The robbers will strip us of our thunder . . .

—So, like a dead letter unanswered,
  Our rococo
  Choir of insects is null
  Cacophony
  And void as a debt summons served
  On a bankrupt;

—But the antiphony, still clamorous,
  In tremolo,
  Like an afternoon, for shadows;
  And the winds
  The distant seven cannons invite us
  To a sonorous

Ishthar's lament for Tammuz:

V

For the far removed there is wailing:

For the far removed;
For the Distant . . .

The wailing is for the fields of crop:

The drums' lament is:
They grow not . . .

The wailing is for the fields of men:

For the barren wedded ones;
For perishing children . . .

The wailing is for the Great River:

Her pot-bellied watchers
Despoil her . . .

*Carving from a Yoruba altar,
representing the spirit of a
king.*

THE PALM-WINE DRINKARD

(Excerpt)

Amos Tutuola

I was a palm-wine drinkard since I was a boy of ten years of age. I had no other work more than to drink palm-wine in my life. In those days we did not know other money, except COWRIES, so that everything was very cheap, and my father was the richest man in our town.

My father got eight children and I was the eldest among them, all of the rest were hard workers, but I myself was an expert palm-wine drinkard. I was drinking palm-wine from morning till night and from night till morning. By that time I could not drink ordinary water at all except palm-wine.

But when my father noticed that I could not do any work more than to drink, he engaged an expert palm-wine tapster for me; he had no other work more than to tap palm-wine every day.

So my father gave me a palm-tree farm, which was nine miles square and it contained 560,000 palm-trees, and this palm-wine tapster was tapping one hundred and fifty kegs of palm-wine every morning, but before 2 o'clock p.m., I would have drunk all of it; after that he would go and tap another 75 kegs in the evening which I would be drinking till morning. So my friends were uncountable by that time and they were drinking palm-wine with me from morning till a late hour in the night. But when my palm-wine tapster completed the period of 15 years that he was tapping the palm-wine for me, then my father died suddenly, and when it was the 6th month after my father had died, the tapster went to the palm-tree farm on a Sunday evening to tap palm-wine for me. When he reached the farm, he climbed one of the tallest palm-trees in the farm to tap palm-wine but as he was tapping on, he fell down unexpectedly and died at the foot of the palm-tree as a result of injuries. As I was waiting for him to bring the palm-wine, when I saw that he did not return in time, because he was not keeping me long like that before, then I called two of my friends to accompany me to the farm. When we reached the farm, we began to look at every palm-tree, after a while we found him under the palm-tree, where he fell down and died.

But what I did first when we saw him dead there, was that I climbed another palm-tree which was near the spot, after that I tapped palm-wine and drank it to my satisfaction before I came back to the spot. Then both my friends who accompanied me to the farm and I dug a pit under the palm-tree that he fell down as a grave and buried him there, after that we came back to the town.

When it was early in the morning of the next day, I had no palm-wine

A palm-wine tapper.

71

to drink at all, and throughout that day I felt not so happy as before; I was seriously sat down in my parlour, but when it was the third day that I had no palm-wine at all, all my friends did not come to my house again, they left me there alone, because there was no palm-wine for them to drink.

But when I completed a week in my house without palm-wine, then I went out and, I saw one of them in the town, so I saluted him, he answered but he did not approach me at all, he hastily went away.

Then I started to find out another expert palm-wine tapster, but I could not get me one who could tap the palm-wine to my requirement. When there was no palm-wine for me to drink I started to drink ordinary water which I was unable to taste before, but I did not satisfy with it as palm-wine.

When I saw that there was no palm-wine for me again, and nobody could tap it for me, then I thought within myself that old people were saying that the whole people who had died in this world, did not go to heaven directly, but they were living in one place somewhere in this world. So that I said that I would find out where my palm-wine tapster who had died was.

One fine morning, I took all my native *ju-ju* and also my father's *ju-ju* with me and I left my father's hometown to find out whereabouts was my tapster who had died.

But in those days, there were many wild animals and every place was covered by thick bushes and forests; again, towns and villages were not near each other as nowadays, and as I was travelling from bushes to bushes and from forests to forests and sleeping inside it for many days and months, I was sleeping on the branches of trees, because spirits etc. were just like partners, and to save my life from them; and again I could spend two or three months before reaching a town or a village. Whenever I reached a town or a village, I would spend almost four months there, to find out my palm-wine tapster from the inhabitants of that town or village and if he did not reach there, then I would leave there and continue my journey to another town or village. After the seventh month that I had left my home town, I reached a town and went to an old man, this old man was not a really man, he was a god and he was eating with his wife when I reached there. When I entered the house I saluted both of them, they answered me well, although nobody should enter his house like that as he was a god, but I myself was a god and *ju-ju*-man. Then I told the old man (god) that I am looking for my palm-wine tapster who had died in my town some time ago, he did not answer to my question but asked me first what was my name? I replied that my name was 'Father of gods' who could do everything in this world, then he said: 'was that true' and I said yes; after that he told me to go to his native black-smith in an unknown place, or who

Treasure box cast in bronze representing the Palace of the Benin Oba.

was living in another town, and bring the right thing that he had told the black-smith to make for him. He said that if I could bring the right thing that he told the black-smith to make for him, then he would believe that I was the 'Father of gods who could do everything in this world' and he would tell me where my tapster was.

Immediately this old man told or promised me so, I went away, but after I had travelled about one mile away then I used one of my *ju-ju* and at once I changed into a very big bird and flew back to the roof of the old man's house; but as I stood on the roof of his house, many people saw me there. They came nearer and looked at me on the roof, so when the old man noticed that many had surrounded his house and were looking at the roof, he and his wife came out from the house and when he saw me (bird) on the roof, he told his wife that if he had not sent me to his native black-smith to bring the bell that he told the black-smith to make for him, he would tell me to mention the name of the bird. But at the same time that he said so, I knew what he wanted from the black-smith and I flew away to his black-smith, then when I reached there I told the black-smith that the old man (god) told me to bring his bell which he had told him to make for him. So the black-smith gave me the bell; after that, I returned to the old man with the bell and when he saw me with the bell, he and his wife were surprised and also shocked at that moment.

After that he told his wife to give me food, but after I had eaten the food, he told me again, that there remained another wonderful work to do for him, before he would tell me whereabouts my tapster was. When it was 6.30 a.m. of the following morning, he (god) woke me up, and gave me a wide and strong net which was the same in colour as the ground of that town. He told me to go and bring 'Death' from his house with the net. When I left his house or the town about a mile, there I saw a junction of roads and I was doubtful when I reached the junction, I did not know which was Death's road among these roads, and when I thought within myself that as it was the market day, and all the market goers would soon be returning from the market—I lied down on the middle of the roads, I put my head to one of the roads, my left hand to one, right hand to another one, and my both feet to the rest, after that I pretended as I had slept there. But when all the market goers were returning from the market, they saw me lied down there and shouted thus: 'Who was the mother of this fine boy, he slept on the roads and put his head towards Death's road.'

Then I began to travel on Death's road, and I spent about eight hours to reach there, but to my surprise I did not meet anybody on this road until I reached there and I was afraid because of that. When I reached his (Death's) house, he was not at home by that time, he was in his yam garden which was very close to his house, and I met a small rolling drum in his verandah, then I beat it to Death as a sign of salutation. But when he (Death) heard the sound of the drum, he said thus: 'Is that man still alive or dead?' Then I replied 'I am still alive and I am not a dead man.'

But at the same time that he heard so from me, he was greatly annoyed and he commanded the drum with a kind of voice that the strings of the drum should tight me there; as a matter of fact, the strings of the drum tighted me so that I was hardly breathing.

When I felt that these strings did not allow me to breathe and again every part of my body was bleeding too much, then I myself commanded the ropes of the yams in his garden to tight him there, and the yam stakes should begin to beat him also. After I had said so and at the same time, all the ropes of the yams in his garden tighted him hardly, and all the yam stakes were beating him repeatedly, so when he (Death) saw that these stakes were beating him repeatedly, then he commanded the strings of the drum which tighted me to release me, and I was released at the same time. But when I saw that I was released, then I myself commanded the ropes of the yams to release him and the yam stakes to stop beating him, and he was released at once. After he was released by the ropes of yams and yam stakes, he came to his house and met me at his verandah, then we shook hands together, and he told me to enter the house, he put me to one of his rooms, and after a while, he brought food to me and we ate it together, after that we started con-

versations which went thus: He (Death) asked me from where did I come? I replied that I came from a certain town which was not so far from this place. Then he asked what did I come to do? I told him that I had been hearing about him in my town and all over the world and I thought within myself that one day I should come and visit or to know him personally. After that he replied that his work was only to kill the people of the world, after that he got up and told me to follow him and I did so.

He took me around his house and his yam garden too, he showed me the skeleton bones of human-beings which he had killed since a century ago and showed me many other things also, but there I saw that he was using skeleton bones of human-beings as fuel woods and skull heads of human-beings as his basins, plates and tumblers etc.

Pair of Yoruba brass casts used for magic and divination.

Nobody was living near or with him there, he was living lonely, even bush animals and birds were very far away from his house. So when I wanted to sleep at night, he gave me a wide black cover cloth and then gave me a separate room to sleep inside, but when I entered the room, I met a bed which was made with bones of human-beings; but as this bed was terrible to look at or to sleep on it, I slept under it instead, because I knew his trick already. Even as this bed was very terrible, I was unable to sleep under as I lied down there because of fear of the bones of human-beings, but I lied down there awoke. To my surprise was that when it was about two o'clock in the mid-night, there I saw somebody enter into the room cautiously with a heavy club in his hands, he came nearer to the bed on which he had told me to sleep, then he clubbed the bed with all his power, he clubbed the centre of the bed thrice and he returned cautiously, he thought that I slept on that bed and he thought also that he had killed me.

But when it was 6 o'clock early in the morning, I first woke up and went to the room in which he slept, I woke him up, so when he heard my voice, he was frightened, even he could not salute me at all when he got up from his bed, because he thought that he had killed me last night.

But the second day that I slept there, he did not attempt to do anything again, but I woke up by two o'clock of that night, and went to the road which I should follow to the town and I travelled about a quarter of a mile to his house, then I stopped and dug a pit of his (Death's) size on the centre of that road, after that I spread the net which the old man gave me to bring him (Death) with on that pit, then I returned to his house, but he did not wake up as I was playing this trick.

When it was 6 o'clock in the morning, I went to his door and woke him up as usual, then I told him that I wanted to return to my town this morning, so that I wanted him to lead me a short distance; then he got up from his bed and he began to lead me as I told him, but when he led me to the place that I had dug, I told him to sit down, so I myself sat down on the road side, but as he sat down on the net, he fell into the pit, and without any ado I rolled up the net with him and put him on my head and I kept going to the old man's house who told me to go and bring him Death.

As I was carrying him along the road, he was trying all his efforts to escape or to kill me, but I did not give him a chance to do that. When I had travelled about eight hours, then I reached the town and went straight to the old man's house who told me to go and bring Death from his house. When I reached the old man's house, he was inside his room, then I called him and told him that I had brought Death that he told me to go and bring. But immediately he heard from me that I had brought Death and when he saw him on my head, he was greatly terrified and raised alarm that he thought nobody could go and bring Death from his house, then he told me to carry him (Death) back to his house at once, and he (old man) hastily went back to his room and started to close all his doors and windows, but before he could close two or three of his windows, I threw down Death before his door and at the same time that I threw him down, the net cut into pieces and Death found his way out.

Then the old man and his wife escaped through the windows and also the whole people in that town ran away for their lives and left their properties there. (The old man had thought that Death would kill me if I went to his house, because nobody could reach Death's house and return, but I had known the old man's trick already.)

So that since the day that I had brought Death out from his house, he has no permanent place to dwell or stay, and we are hearing his name about in the world. This was how I brought out Death to the old man who told me to go and bring him before he (old man) would tell me whereabouts my palm-wine tapster was that I was looking for before I reached that town and went to the old man.

But the old man who had promised me that if I could go to Death's house and bring him, he would tell me whereabouts my palm-wine tapster was, could not wait and fulfil his promise because he himself and his wife were narrowly escaped from that town.

Then I left the town without knowing where my tapster was, and I started another fresh journey.

Palm-wine jugs from a nineteenth-century engraving.

Bronze plate from the Benin Palace showing messenger of death.

ABIKU

Wole Soyinka

Abiku is the Yoruba myth of infant mortality, meaning literally, 'born-to-die'. It is believed that the dead child returns to plague the mother.

In vain your bangles cast
Charmed circles at my feet.
I am Abiku, calling for the first
And repeated time.

Must I weep for goats and cowries,
For palm oil and the sprinkled ash?
Yams do not sprout in armlets
To earth Abiku's limbs.

So when the snail is burnt in his shell
With the heated fragment, brand me
Deeply on the breast. You must know him
When Abiku calls again.

I am the squirrel teeth, cracked.
The riddle of the palm. Remember
This and dig me deeper still into
The god's swollen foot.

Once and the repeated time
Ageless though I puke. And when
You pour libations, each finger
Points me near the way I came, where

The ground is wet with mourning,
White dew suckles flesh-birds,
Evening befriends the spider,
Trapping flies in wine-froth.

Night, and Abiku sucks the oil
From lamps. Mothers! I'll be the
Suppliant snake coiled on the doorstep,
Yours the killing cry.

The ripest fruit was saddest.
Where I crept, the warmth was cloying.
In the silence of webs Abiku moans
Shaping mounds from the yolk.

Yoruba food container.

THE SULTAN OF BORNOU

Dixon Denham

17 February. This was to us a momentous day, and it seemed to be equally so to our conductors. Notwithstanding all the difficulties that had presented themselves at the various stages of our journey, we were at last within a few short miles of our destination; were about to become acquainted with a people who had never seen, or scarcely heard of, a European; and to tread on ground, the knowledge and true situation of which had hitherto been wholly unknown. These ideas of course excited no common sensations; and could scarcely be unaccompanied by strong hopes of our labours being beneficial to the race amongst whom we were shortly to mix; of our laying the first stone of a work which might lead to their civilization, if not their emancipation from all their prejudices and ignorance, and probably, at the same time, open a field of commerce to our own country, which might increase its wealth and prosperity. Our accounts had been so contradictory of the state of this country, that no opinion could be formed as to the real condition or the numbers of its inhabitants. We had been told that the sheikh's soldiers were a few ragged negroes armed with spears, who lived upon the plunder of the Black Kaffir countries, by which he was surrounded, and which he was enabled to subdue by the assistance of a few Arabs who were in his service; and, again, we had been assured that his forces were not only numerous, but to a certain degree well trained. The degree of credit which might be attached to these reports was nearly balanced in the scales of probability; and we advanced towards the town of Kouka in a most interesting state of uncertainty, whether we should find its chief at the head of thousands, or be received by him under a tree, surrounded by a few naked slaves.

These doubts, however, were quickly removed. I had ridden on a short distance in front of Boo-Khaloom, with his train of Arabs, all mounted, and dressed out in their best apparel; and, from the thickness of the trees, soon lost sight of them, fancying that the road could not be mistaken. I rode still onwards, and on approaching a spot less thickly planted, was not a little surprised to see in front of me a body of several thousand cavalry drawn up in line, and extending right and left quite as far as I could see; and, checking my horse, I awaited the arrival of my party, under the shade of a wide-spreading acacia. The Bornou troops remained quite steady, without noise or confusion; and a few horsemen, who were moving about in front giving directions, were the only persons out of the ranks. On the Arabs appearing in sight, a shout, or yell, was given by the sheikh's people, which rent the air: a blast was blown from their rude instruments of music equally loud, and they moved on to meet Boo-Khaloom and his Arabs. There was an appearance of tact and management in their movements which astonished me: three separate small bodies, from the centre and each flank, kept charging rapidly towards us, to within a few feet of our horses' heads, without checking the speed of their own until the moment of their halt, while the whole body moved onwards. These parties were mounted on small but very perfect horses, who stopped, and wheeled from their utmost speed with great precision and expertness, shaking their spears over their heads, exclaiming *'Barca! barca! Alla hiak kum cha, alla cheraga!* —Blessing! blessing! Sons of your country! Sons of your country!' and returning quickly to the front of the body in order to repeat the charge. While all this was going on, they closed in their right and left flanks, and surrounded the little body of Arab warriors so completely, as to give the compliment of welcoming them very much the appearance of a declaration of their contempt for their weakness . . .

The sheikh's negroes, as they were called, meaning the black chiefs and favourites, all raised to that rank by some deed of bravery, were habited in coats of mail composed of iron chain, which covered them from the throat to the knees, dividing behind, and coming on each side of the horse: some of them had helmets, or rather skull caps, of the same metal, with chin pieces, all sufficiently strong to ward off the shock of a spear. Their horses' heads were also defended by plates of iron, brass and silver, just leaving sufficient room for the eyes of the animal.

*

Our huts were immediately so crowded with visitors, that we had not a moment's peace, and the heat was insufferable. Boo-Khaloom had delivered his presents from the bashaw, and brought us a message of compliment, together with an intimation that our own would be received on the following day. About noon we received a summons to attend the sheikh; and we proceeded to the palace, preceded by our negroes, bearing the articles destined for the sheikh by our government; consisting of a double-barrelled gun, by Wilkinson, with a box, and all the apparatus complete, a pair of excellent pistols in a case, two pieces of superfine broad cloth, red and blue, to which we added a set of china, and two bundles of spices.

The ceremony of getting into the presence was ridiculous enough, although nothing could be more plain and devoid of pretension than the appearance of the sheikh himself. We passed through passages lined with attendants, the front men sitting on their hams; and when we advanced too quickly, we were suddenly arrested by these fellows, who caught forcibly hold us of by the legs, and had not the crowd prevented

A bodyguard of the Sheikh of Bornou, from a sketch by Major Dixon Denham.

our falling, we should most infallibly have become prostrate before arriving in the presence. Previous to entering into the open court, in which we were received, our papouches, or slippers, were whipped off by these active though sedentary gentlemen of the chamber; and we were seated on some clean sand on each side of a raised bench of earth, covered with a carpet, on which the sheikh was reclining. We laid the gun and the pistols together before him, and explained to him the locks, turnscrews, and steel shot-cases holding two charges each, with all of which he seemed exceedingly well pleased: the powder-flask, and the manner in which the charge is divided from the body of powder, did not escape his observation; the other articles were taken off by the slaves, almost as soon as they were laid before him. Again we were questioned as to the object of our visit. The sheikh, however, showed evident satisfaction at our assurance that the king of England had heard of Bornou and himself; and, immediately turning to his kaganawha (counsellor), said, 'This is in consequence of our defeating the Beg-harmis.' Upon which, the chief who had most distinguished himself in these memorable battles, Bagah Furby (the gatherer of horses) seating himself in front of us, demanded, 'Did he ever hear of me?' The imme-diate reply of 'Certainly' did wonders for our cause. Exclamations were general; and, 'Ah! then, your king must be a great man!' was re-echoed from every side. We had nothing offered us by way of refreshment, and took our leave.

I may here observe, that besides occasional presents of bullocks, camel-loads of wheat and rice, leathern skins of butter, jars of honey, and honey in the comb, five or six wooden bowls were sent us, morning and evening, containing rice, with meat, paste made of barley flour, savoury but very greasy; and on our first arrival, as many had been sent of sweets, mostly composed of curd and honey.

In England a brace of trout might be considered as a handsome present to a traveller sojourning in the neighbourhood of a stream, but at Bornou things are done differently. A camel-load of bream, and a sort of mullet, was thrown before our huts on the second morning after our arrival; and for fear that should not be sufficient, in the evening another was sent.

THE INTERPRETERS

(Excerpt)

Wole Soyinka

Monica Faseyi was always in disgrace. And so at the entrance to the embassy reception her husband stopped and inspected her thoroughly. Satisfied, he nodded and quickly checked the line of his own bow-tie. He smiled then and kissed her formally on the forehead.

'You might as well put on your gloves now.'

'What gloves? I didn't bring any.'

Faseyi thought she was teasing, and out of character though it was, Monica was certain that her husband was teasing.

'Come on now, put on the gloves.'

'You stop teasing, now. Who do you see wearing gloves in Nigeria?'

Faseyi was no longer joking. He had snatched the handbag from her and found that there were no gloves inside. 'Do you mean you didn't bring them?'

'Bring what, Ayo?'

'The gloves, of course. What else?'

'But I haven't any gloves. I gave the ones I had away soon after I came.'

'I am not talking about two years ago. I mean the gloves you've bought for tonight.'

'I didn't buy any. Ayo, what's all this?'

'What's all this? I should ask you what's all this! Didn't I give you an invitation over a week ago?'

'Yes you did, but . . .'

'Darling, I gave you a cheque for fifteen pounds to get yourself all you needed.'

'I thought you wanted me to have a new dress.'

'For heaven's sake, what about the gloves?'

'But you didn't say anything about gloves.'

'Was it necessary to say anything? It was right there on the card. In black and white.' He took the card from his pocket, dragged it from the envelope and thrust it under her eyes. 'Read it, there it is. Read it.'

Monica read the last line on the card. 'But Ayo, it only says those who are to be presented. We are not, are we?'

Ayo held his head. 'We are to be presented.'

'You didn't tell me. How was I to know?'

'How were you to know! It took me two weeks to wangle the presentation, and now you ask me how were you to know. What would be the whole point of coming if we were not to be presented?'

'I am sorry,' said Monica, 'it never occurred to me . . .'

'Nothing ever occurs to you!'

Bandele and Kola continued to hug the shadows where they had gone for fresh air, unwilling eavesdroppers, but it was too late to move.

'Do you know them?'

'Ayo Faseyi, Teaching Hospital.'

The emphasis shifted somewhat, Faseyi saying, 'But at least you could have used some initiative. Even if there was no question of being presented, you knew Their Excellencies would be here.'

'I am sorry.'

'Darling, if the Queen was attending a garden party, would you go dressed without your gloves?'

'I've said I am sorry, Ayo. I really am. Perhaps I had better return home.'

'But would you? Answer my question. Would you attend the same party with the Queen without gloves.'

'I really don't know, Ayo. I never moved in such circles.'

'Darling, I am surprised at you. These are simple requirements of society which any intelligent person would know.' He looked at his watch, thinking rapidly, biting his lips in vexation. And then he hit a solution. 'Of course, Mummy will help out. She is bound to have a pair at home.'

The young girl with the mild voice said, 'No, Ayo. It's much simpler for me just to go back home.'

'What is the use if I cannot be presented with my wife? Let's go back for the gloves.'

'The reception will be over by the time we get back.'

The thought halted Faseyi definitely. 'All right, come on. But you will have to stay behind when we are called.'

'Of course. I am really sorry this happened, Ayo.'

They went in, and Bandele and Kola were released from their long restriction.

'Some domestic scene.'

Bandele sighed. 'I'm going to be told all about it tomorrow.'

'Who by?'

'Faseyi. I know him very well.'

'Oh, is it a regular thing?'

'Once for every social occasion at least, including their own at-homes.'

'It's going to rain.' Kola brushed off a drop on his arm.

'When did it ever stop?'

'What has happened anyway? The season used to be more precise. And four months at the most. Maybe five.'

'Bommmmmmmbs.' Bandele, with his deepest bass.

'Last week I felt suddenly starved for some flare of colours so I woke up early to see in the dawn. And it came, by God it came. A huge suspension of *ewedu*.'

84

'Come on, let's get in from it.'

Sagoe, locked with the ambassador, full of virtue in the course of duty, had immersed himself in a borrowed dinner jacket, and there was nothing of the journalist in his appearance. Sagoe, desperate. Between him and an 'exclusive statement' lay years of trained caution and it would not be lulled.

'At that time we were all full of the propaganda, "secret of life discovered by Stalin's doctors". A special plasma extracted from live children, and each injection made Stalin younger by ten years. Stalin could never die—they said.'

'Well,' the ambassador spoke slowly, 'I would agree—in a sense— with that. Stalin, like other dictators, did purchase longevity with human lives. So did Hitler. But it is in the nature of dictators to be rather . . . predatory on human beings.'

'I agree, sir. But still you believe that a dictatorship is often the most sensible government for a nation?'

'It depends on the nation, as I said before.'

'If I may use yours as an example, don't you agree sir, that . . .'

'Ah, will you excuse me a moment, Mr Sagoe. I must welcome the new guests . . .'

Sagoe charged into Kola and Bandele just outside the door in his headlong rush out. 'What's eating him?'

'He couldn't have got his story. Hey, Sagoe, wait . . .'

'I'll see you back at the house,' he shouted back.

'He must have been pretty well frustrated. He didn't even wait to get drunk.'

The ambassador approached the Faseyis accompanied by a waiter bearing a trayload of champagne. Monica shook her head, and already Faseyi looked displeased. The ambassador was hospitably incredulous. 'But don't you drink at all, Mrs Faseyi?' 'No, only the occasional palm wine when our steward feels kindly towards us.' The ambassador laughed and gestured regretfully. 'I am so sorry, I really wish we had palm wine.'

One of the waiters was passing with more champagne and overheard. Faseyi had wandered off to seek the Master of Presentations; when he returned, Monica had a glass of palm wine in her hand, and a colleague of Faseyi was asking, 'What have you got there, Monica? Mist alba?'

'Where did you get that?' Faseyi shouted.

'One of the stewards brought it. He overheard us talk about palm wine and went to fetch it from his house. Wasn't that sweet of him?'

Faseyi went scrambling towards Bandele. 'You see, she has begun again.'

Bandele wore his mask of infinite patience. 'What has she done now?'

'It was bad enough to refuse the champagne, although mind you I just don't see any necessity for it. After all, how many of these women here touch their drink? They just hold the glass in their hand to be sociable, what is wrong with that?'

Kola murmured, 'Nothing, nothing, I'm sure.'

Faseyi looked at him with love and gratitude. 'But you see, that isn't all. She wasn't satisfied with that. She had to go and ask for palm wine at a cocktail reception. Have you ever heard such a thing? For palm wine!'

Bandele's grave aspect consoled him not at all.

'If she were a bush-girl from some London slum I could understand. But she is educated. She has moved in society. Why does she have to come and disgrace me by drinking palm wine?'

'Oh' Kola looked concerned. 'You mean she even got it?'

Faseyi spun round. 'Look at her if you don't believe me. There she is over there, drinking palm wine if you please. And someone even came along as I saw her, and I bet he is spreading the story all over the place already.'

'Oh, he may not know it was palm wine.'

'He did. He was even sneering. Is that mist alba? that's what he said.'

'You should have said yes,' Kola told him. 'After all it would be more understandable that your wife was taken suddenly ill and had to have some mist alba.'

'Yes . . . I suppose so . . . I suppose so. I should have thought of it. But the trouble is Monica. She would have made some careless slip and given herself away. Look, Bandele, be a friend. If you hear any adverse comments, let me know, will you. Much better if one knew what people are saying in time, then one can do something about it. And also . . .' Faseyi drew closer and whispered, 'about her dress.'

Bandele said, 'What are you talking about?'

'Don't you see she is improperly dressed?'

'I hadn't noticed.'

In Faseyi's eyes a sudden gleam of hope. 'You mean you hadn't? Well that's a relief, perhaps most people won't either.'

'I am afraid you are wrong,' Kola said.

'Oh. So you've noticed.'

Kola improved on it. 'Not me. I don't know much about clothes. But I heard a group over there commenting on her.'

Turning to Bandele. 'You see!'

'I wouldn't pay much attention,' Kola continued. 'You get these spiteful types everywhere, and those ones were'—and a doleful shake of the head—'anyway I don't need to tell you. You know how catty people can be.'

'No, no, it's not cattiness. They are quite right. Look, what did they say exactly?'

Bandele interfered and manœuvred Faseyi away and towards his wife. They had hardly come to Monica before Faseyi burst out 'You see how conspicuous you've made us? Look around and see for yourself. Even those in native dress are wearing gloves.'

Bandele withdrew at the first decent opportunity, returning to attack an unrepentant Kola. 'What were all those lies in aid of?'

'The man likes to worry. I only helped him with material.'

Bandele shook his head. 'Don't waste your sympathy on Monica. I know both of them.'

'It is not a question of sympathy.'

'She sounds mild but she isn't. In fact I have still to meet a tougher girl.'

'She looks very young.'

An official, the 'Master of Presentations', moved among the guests with a list, taking the chosen few and leading them to their brief fulfilment, and Faseyi followed him with side-glances. Calculating along the alphabet when his turn approached, he moved away and joined Bandele again. The ruse was obvious to Monica and she lowered her head into the palm wine, pretending not to see.

'Ah there you are, Mr Faseyi. Will you bring your wife and come with me please.'

'Oh my wife is . . . er . . . she is rather shy. I'll have to go by myself.'

'Nonsense, we can't have that sort of thing. Let me talk to her.'

'No, no, no, it's no use believe me. I've done nothing else but try and persuade her all evening. Let's go and get it over with.'

A few moments later, Bandele tugged Kola by the sleeve. 'Look!'

'Your Excellencies, may I present . . . oh . . . that's better, you screwed up your courage at last . . . beg pardon, Your Excellencies, may I now present Mr and Mrs Faseyi, University Teaching Hospital.'

Kola's face was all screwed up in perplexity. 'Just what is the matter with your friend?'

'He is supposed to be the best X-ray analyst available in the continent.'

'Is that supposed to be of some relevance?'

Bandele shrugged.

Faseyi stomped out, Monica in his wake, as soon as the presentation was over. Five minutes later he returned by himself.

RECIPE FOR KOLA

Sir Richard Burton

The Shaykh then presented me with a handful of kola nuts,[1] which have been called the African coffee. They are the local 'chaw', the succedaneum for tobacco, betel nut, mastick, and sweet earth. The tree, which grows everywhere in the damp and wooded regions of the tropical seaboard, and on the islands of West Africa (where, however, the people ignore its use), is a kind of sterculia, in leaf not unlike the magnolia, but a stunted scrubby tree; the flower is small and white, with a polypetalous corolla, and the fruit is a large pod, like a misshapen cucumber. The edible parts are the five or six beans, which are compared to Brazilian nuts, and to horse chestnuts; they are covered with a pure white placenta, which must be removed with the finger-nails, and then appears the rosy pink skin—some varieties are yellow—which gradually becomes rusty by exposure to the air. The nut is easily divided into several, generally four sections, of which one is eaten at a time. The taste is a pleasant bitter, and somewhat astringent. Water drunk 'upon it', as the phrase is, becomes, even if before offensive, exceptionally sweet. It must be a fine tonic in these relaxing climates. I am not aware of an extract having been made from it: if not, it would be as well to try. Travellers use it to quiet the sensation of hunger and to obviate thirst. In native courts eating kola nuts forms part of the ceremony of welcoming strangers, and the Yorubas have a proverb: 'Anger draweth arrows from the quiver: good words draw kolas from the bag.' It is held to be aphrodisiac—of these half the African, like the Asiatic, pharmacopeia is composed—and like the betel to be 'A detergent, and a kindler of Love's flame that lieth dead'.

A powder, or an infusion of the bark and leaves, promptly administered, is used on the Gold Coast as a cure of snake bites. There, also, kola powders finely ground are drunk in a wineglassful of limejuice by those who do not wish to become mothers. And a decoction of the leaves, like the terebinthinate palm vine, acts as a substitute for copaiba.

Two girl students. (Photo Marc Riboud, MAGNUM)

---

[1] The Kola (Sterculia acuminata) is written in many ways—Cola, Colat, Khola, Gura, Goera, and Gooroo; the latter three are the names given by the older travellers.

THE GIRLS OF LAGOS

(Excerpt from Iska*)*

Cyprian Ekwensi

The city is a girl walking
    walking at dawn
handbag over arm,
    heels down and hungry
Walking at noon
    hunger in the vitals
Walking at dusk
bracelets all aglitter
    heels high and flattering
The city is a girl walking
    into offices
adventuring into bedrooms
seducing into the top
The city is a girl walking
    ever walking
    ever scheming
    ever climbing
  climbing into cockpits
  climbing up to heights
  where only girls can climb
Who can sit back and ignore
light skin girl along the street
all make-up from wig to nail paint
head held high and bosom taut
rear end wiggling, calculating, tantalizing
Eyes afire with a dare-me challenge
Seems the world is hers
And the city is a haven
For girls always walking
upsetting the traffic
disturbing the office
pressing male faces
against working windows
creating sensation
commanding attention
In an Africa for men
The city is a girl walking . . .
    Always walking . . .'

90

A WREATH FOR THE MAIDENS

(Excerpt)

John Munonye

There was a terrific storm during the night. Without doubt it was the worst for years, raging for hours on end and featuring thunder claps and lightning flashes and violent winds.

It began with distant rumblings and responses, like the echo of explosions in a sustained artillery duel. Then a wild wind rose carrying all with it, including sand and dry leaves, and a drizzle. Finally, the rain started pouring in a thick mass; and the earth, sprayed with cold, liquid bullets, began to bleed. The flood, fast and brown, flowed through the paths, into the fields, submerging the crops. Up above, lightning flashes tore open the heavens again and again. Between such flashes, thunder would boom, and the sound would bounce through space, reaching the earth with unnerving reverberations.

All that was before the hour of dawn, and now, the sun had taken control once again.

I rose from the bed, slouched over to the backyard, thoughtfully, chewing-stick in mouth, the leg-ends of my pyjama-trousers sweeping the ground after me. It was an attractively bright morning, with a clear view ahead, even beyond the large cassava plot which adjoined the school compound.

There was a palm-tree at the centre of the plot. Tall grass with richly tasselled apexes encircled the tree, to a height of about eight feet. A squadron of birds, darting across the plot, perched on the grass and began to peck. They were very small and very clever with their beaks as well as with their wings; and they had a most serene combination of colours in their plumage, including a frontal white, like a waistcoat, or a tabard, and a blue rear.

These birds were definitely enjoying themselves, I reflected. And then, as if they had just read my mind, some of them went off to demonstrate: they careened, wheeled, and finally returned to base. Some others went on frisking and preening themselves. And others chirruped. From time to time, they dug their beaks into the stems, and into the tassels, of the grass.

A palm-nut detaching itself from the branch overhead fell on the ground with a thud. The birds flew away, but only to return a few moments later when they had sensed that the danger was by no means real. A gentle wind blew and the grass swayed, dully. Apart from that, the cassava plot lay still.

It was almost three months now since Chimara and her daughters had put the cassava into the soil. I still remembered how she had stood, leaning against her stick and supervising while her four daughters, all married, did the planting. The plants were some two to three feet high now, and the leaves had that lush appearance which was a sure promise of rich harvest. Or rather, that was so up to the day before. This morning, most of the plants had drooping branches, because of the storm.

Old Chimara was there already, I exclaimed in my mind, still gazing into the distance. Yes, it was she, so early in the day. Going from one line to another, Chimara tried to raise some of the plants which had fallen victim to the onslaught. 'Get up; go on!' I heard her urge with strength. 'Get up; the storm is over.' She applied her walking stick this time, with maternal art. 'Get up, please,' Chimara pleaded. 'Your life is not ended.'

There was a child close by at her side. He was her grandson. He moaned: 'Mother, this one is dead.'

'Dead? No,' she protested. 'But don't hurt it.' Then, still bending double and supporting herself with the stick, she went over to the spot, where the child had already plucked off the leaves, leaving only the bare stem. 'Show me,' she inquired.

'Mother, here.' Hiding the leaves behind his back with guilt, he pointed with the remaining hand.

She gave an unearthly chuckle. 'Emenike, this is what you call death, is it? No, my son; it may still live.' She drew closer; and she shook it gently. 'It is only weak. Some have died, it's true, but not this one.'

'Mother, why is it weak?' Emenike asked.

'Because of the storm, my son,' she replied.

'What did the storm do to it?'

'It twisted it. And then,' she added, 'somebody came and plucked off the leaves. The roots are still there and therefore it will not die. It is the roots which are its soul.'

'Ah—ah—ah!' the child exclaimed, greatly impressed. 'So if the roots die it will die?''

'That's so,' she answered mechanically.

I whistled a song, merely to warn them about my presence, then moved closer until I had come to the fence between.

'Mother, I greet you,' I called.

'My good son!' came her response.

'You are well?'

'Well? Yes; your mother may be said to be well.' She paused. 'But what does my being well matter, seeing that I am a setting sun?'

Puzzled, I asked: 'Has anything happened?'

'Whether anything has happened?' she asked after yet another ominous pause. 'These things one is hearing of late about people being killed make one sick—sick on behalf of the young. And you know, my son, last night's storm was only a sign from the gods.' She turned round abruptly, indicating that she had become uncommunicative.

The lush growth of the countryside near Benin City

92

THE PARADOX

Francesca Yetunde Pereira

      The cross, the icon
      The disciples fought
      They are still fighting
      The whiteman claims
      His god supreme
      And blackman muses
White god, in reason can I hope for grace bestowed,
The disciples fought. They are still fighting, maybe
Somewhere in white clouds, somewhere in blackest
Abyss, the white god and the black god dumb,
      Look silently on.
      The disciples fought
      They all of them join
      Battle, fierce raging,
      Each god is mighty.
They must be. It must be. The world is constant in its chaos.
The world is crumbling and all gods are silent. Evil begets
Good begets evil. Watching. Wenching Eves, empty headed apes
Demanding, exacting. Their folly drowning in spirits flowing.
      And the Infant, crying
      For the dried-up stream
      The lapped-up stream
      Caked stream of life
      Is milked in a manger
      Sawdust and straw.
      Cool breeze fleeting
      Past suspense, hope,
      And prophecy. Empty.
The age old tree without, magnificent, proudly stands
Its yellowing leaves waft to and fro against the deep
Blue sky. The mind persists in calmness, and frenzy
Beats a wild resounding drum within the tortured heart.
      Learn patience
      O frenzied drumbeat
      Be still and rein
      Thyself. Advent of
      Destiny. Wildly yours.
      Then canst thou beat

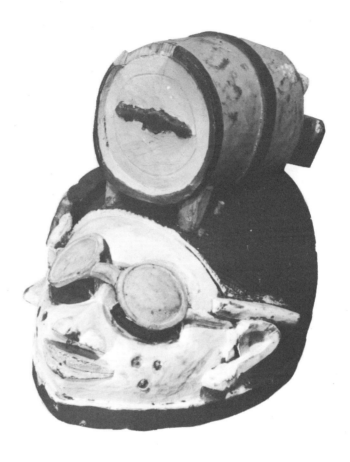

Dance mask of the Gelede society representing the spirit of the white man, in sun glasses and with a rum barrel on his head.

Wild wild refrain
And drum and dance
For joy. Or rend
Dumb heavens with
Thy woes. The age
Old tree, the cheery
Room, the bright blue
Sky above. The drum
Still blind, beats on.
The fevered drum still blind beats wildly fiercely on.
No crumbs fall from the orgies of the rich. Eves and apes
With licentious smell trampling the earth.
Under their feet the bones of infants. Disciples still
Fighting. Each god is mighty. The world is crumbling. And gods
    are silent.

95

EFURU

(Excerpt)

Flora Nwapa

Ajanupu took the dead child in her arms and looked at it closely. Tears rolled down her cheeks. Up to the time Ajanupu arrived, Efuru did not know exactly what had happened. Then she saw tears on Ajanupu's cheeks and she realized that her only child was dead. She threw herself on the floor of the room and wept hysterically.

Ogea ran out, put her two hands in both ears and shouted: 'Our people, come, come: Ogonim is dead. Ogonim the only child of Efuru is dead.' Neighbours ran to Efuru's house. Ajanupu was still holding the dead child. Tears were still rolling down her cheeks. Efuru was rolling on the floor. The first woman to arrive took the child from Ajanupu.

'Why, she is not dead. Don't you see that her body is warm. She is still alive.'

Ajanupu hissed:

'Give her to me. Don't you see? Have you eyes and you don't see? Don't you see that she is dead?' Ajanupu snatched the dead child from the woman. She put her on her lap again and began to look at her as before. 'Ogonim, so you have gone. So you refused to stay with us. You are a foolish child to leave all the wealth and riches for the land of the dead. You are ungrateful for leaving your good mother. A mother who is more than all mothers. A good mother in the real sense of goodness. You saw the wealth, the riches, good home and you chose the life in the other world. You have not done well, my daughter.'

Ogea wept in her corner. She went to her mistress and placed her hands on her lap. 'Mama, Ogonim has wronged us. Ogonim has not done well. What will you do? What am I going to do? Who am I going to look after? Oh, Ogonim, why did you treat us like this?'

Efuru's mother-in-law wept softly at her corner. There were no tears. She was not given to much talk. Throughout her life, she had been to herself a symbol of suffering. These self-imposed sufferings had sobered her. Now, nothing excited her. She even found it difficult to produce tears from her eyes. She had shed so many tears that it did not seem as if there were any more tears for her to shed. But watching her in her corner, anybody could see that she was in great grief.

Efuru was still rolling on the floor. Sometimes she would take Ogonim from Ajanupu, look at her, shake her head and hand her back to Ajanupu. She called on the gods to bear witness. She raised her hands and asked the gods and her ancestors where and when she offended them that they should allow her only child to be snatched by death.

'Let's not sit down doing nothing,' Ajanupu said, getting up from the floor. 'Ogonim's father must be sent for, the corpse will be buried and there are sympathizers to be looked after. Ossai, get up and be useful. This is early morning. Go down to the stream and see if there are people going to Ndoni and give them a message for Adizua. Be quick, please. You will find many people going to Ndoni today being Eke day.'

'But will his "wife" allow him to come home?' Ajanupu thought. 'Men are such queer people. They are so weak that when they are under the thumb of a woman, she does whatever she likes with them. And that woman? That devil in the form of a woman, she won't allow him to come home and bury his only child. I can see the subtle way she would do it. I can imagine her now saying that she is expecting a baby, and pretending to be very ill, and Adizua putting off homecoming every day until it is too late to come home. But why think about this now, when there is so much to be done?' she thought.

Efuru was too tired and confused to be of much use. Ogea had the corpse now, she was still weeping but this time very softly. She was so grown up now. 'Ogea, put her down on the bare floor. The floor is cool and the coolness will preserve the corpse. Now go and get some water from the stream. When you return, leave it at the back of the house,' Ajanupu said.

When Ogea went to the stream, Ajanupu swept the floor. She carried the bed from the bedroom to the sitting-room and spread a beautiful velvet cloth on it. She went to the mud wardrobe and brought out some mats with beautiful designs and spread them on the mud-benches for sympathizers. 'Now Efuru, tie your cloth well and come out and sit down in the sitting-room. You cannot stay in the room for you will faint for want of air. Get up, my daughter, and come with me.' Ajanupu supported Efuru as she left the bedroom for the sitting-room. 'Now sit down at this corner. You will be able to recognize sympathizers when they come. Now be brave about it. Don't weep too much for you will be ill afterwards. Remember that Ogonim has gone and gone for ever. No amount of weeping will bring her back to life.'

Neighbours and sympathizers were now arriving. Mats were spread outside for them to sit down. Ajanupu went to the back of the house and there she washed Ogonim thoroughly. Ogea brought out a new dress for the corpse, and showed it to Ajanupu.

'Show it to her mother first,' Ajanupu said.

When Ogea showed it to Efuru, she shook her head and beckoned Ogea to come nearer. Then Ogea went to the mud wardrobe—the room in a room, very dark both in the daytime and at night. The mud wardrobe was used for storing valuable things—boxes of clothes, jars, ornaments, iron pots and jewellery. If the house caught fire, the things in the mud wardrobe would not have been burnt. The top of the mud wardrobe was used as a shelf for odd things like mats, cooking-pots, soups, boxes and brooms. When policemen came to search for home-made gin it was hidden away in the mud wardrobe for policemen did not know there were such things as mud wardrobes.

In this wardrobe, Efuru put her most valuable things of all, like the ornaments she had inherited from her mother and rich clothes of different kinds. Ogea entered the mud wardrobe and struggled out with a heavy box. She put it down, opened it and brought out a dress made of damask material. 'This is the one Ogonim's mother wants her to wear,' she told Ajanupu. Ajanupu took it from her and put it on the dead child. Then she powdered her face and sprinkled some perfume on her. After this, she carried her reverently to the bed which she had already prepared. Then she moved a step backwards and surveyed the corpse, the little body lying in state. It was a human being that was full of life only three days ago, now it was a corpse. If it was not buried by the time the sun went down, it would stink, and sympathizers would flee from the place. As she looked at the little body, Ajanupu began to weep all over again. 'You wanted to leave us, and you have left us. So good-bye, my child.'

Efuru's mother-in-law came in. She was surprised to see that Ajanupu had washed the corpse and dressed it. She tapped Ajanupu on the shoulder. She turned and followed her into the room.

'I have sent messages through different people going to Ndoni. In two days' time, our message will reach Ndoni and Adizua should arrive in four days' time.'

'That's all right. Let's perform the sacrifices expected of us, and let the gods take any blame.'

'You are right, my sister,' Efuru's mother-in-law said to her sister. 'You are perfectly right. We must do our bit so that we are not accused of negligence.'

Sympathizers poured in in great numbers and wept on the feet of Efuru one after the other. The sitting-room was full and mats were spread outside for them to sit down. A distant relation of Efuru came and fell on her feet. 'Efuru,' she began very slowly. 'I am very sorry. I am indeed very sorry. So all your sufferings have come to naught. Efuru, in what ways have you offended our ancestors? What is the reason for this—a child who was more than two years old. You were married and for a long time you did not have a child. Then our gods and the ancestors opened your womb and you had a baby girl. We all rejoiced for you. A girl is something, though we would have preferred a boy. You looked after your child very well, feeding her and nursing her. And now, that only child is dead. And you have suffered for nothing. So you have come to the world to suffer?

'As if all this is not enough for a child like you to bear,' the woman went on. 'I hear your husband has run away with that worthless woman, the daughter of a bitch. He has left you to bear the burden alone. The world is strange. Adizua who was nobody before you married him. Adizua whose father roamed the length and breadth of the Great River and later on died of a bad disease. And you the daughter of Nwashike Ogene, a man of noble parentage. A man who is upright and whose ancestors were upright and just.

'Leave everything to the gods and our ancestors, my daughter. God will heal your wounds and our gods will visit Adizua and the woman who . . .'

'That will do,' Ajanupu shouted from the room. 'That will do, I say. What nonsense. Nwasobi, if you don't know how to sympathize with a woman whose only child has died, say you are sorry and leave her in peace, and don't stay there enumerating all her misfortunes in a tone that suggests that you enjoy these misfortunes.'

'Ajanupu, you are right,' said a woman. 'I have never seen anything like that before. Nwasobi, don't talk like that any more. When you go, Efuru will think of all you have said and will be more miserable.'

The woman was embarrassed, she got up. 'I am sorry, my daughter. Please pardon me. We are old women and therefore know nothing.'

Efuru was quiet. She did not say a word to anybody. She did not even hear Nwasobi when she was blabbing like a woman possessed. When the woman said she was sorry, she simply nodded. Ajanupu watched her all the time. She saw that she was thinking very much and that was bad for her health. And what was more she was not crying any more. It was better to shed tears than to restrain them from flowing freely. One feels better after shedding tears, for tears sometimes have a soothing effect.

'My daughter,' Ajanupu said to Efuru placing her hands on her shoulders. 'My daughter, please weep, weep, my daughter, weeping will do you good. Don't stay like that without weeping. Weep! Let your tears flow freely. If you don't weep, your heart will be injured.'

'I cannot weep any more, Ajanupu. My grief is the kind of grief that allows no tears. It is a dry grief. Wet grief is better but I cannot weep.'

'No, my child, try and weep. Tears wash away sorrows. Your burden is made lighter if you weep. Women weep easily and that is why they do not feel sorrows as keenly as men do.'

'Ajanupu, my daughter has killed me. Ogonim has killed me. My only child has killed me. Why should I live? I should be dead too and lie in state beside my daughter. Oh, my chi, why have you dealt with me in this way?' When Efuru said this tears rolled down her cheeks.

'That's better, my child. Weep,' Ajanupu encouraged.

There was a shout from a distance.

'My people, come and see me, come round and see my friend Efuru and her only child. I am lost. I am done for. What am I hearing?' The shout of this new sympathizer cut through the silence of that serene morning, the morning that brought doom and darkness to Efuru.

'Who can that be?' Ajanupu asked irritatingly. 'She is not going to say nonsense here like that other woman.'

The new sympathizer was one of Efuru's friends, the woman who had painted fearsome pictures of nursemaids and had advised Efuru not to have anything to do with them.

'Efuru, my friend,' she said and fell on her feet. 'Efuru, sorry, I am very sorry. I saw Ogonim hale and hearty only three days ago. She and Ogea were returning from Ajanupu's place. She had a banana and when I asked her to give me the banana she gave it to me. I thanked her and gave her back the banana and she smiled at me. It was such a sweet smile. What killed that healthy child? A child whose other name was life itself, how did death get at her? Sorry my dear friend. Have heart and don't worry. God knows best.'

When she finished, she went to the little corpse and began to talk to her.

'Ogonim, the daughter of my friend, the daughter of Efuru and Adizua. Why have you treated my friend in this way? Did we not treat you well? Why have you left us? Where are you going? Is it as good as this place?'

She got up and went and sat at a corner. A fairly elderly woman got up from her corner and went to Efuru. 'Efuru I am going. Nobody owns this world. Death does not know how to kill. Death visits everybody, the rich, the poor, the blind and the lame. When it visits us, it seems as if our own grief and loss are more than our neighbours'. I conceived eight times. All died before they were six months old. The last one was a girl and when she did not die after six months, I killed a white fowl for my chi. I named her Ibiakwa—Have you come again? After a year and she did not die I called her Nkem—My own. She was a beautiful girl, she shone like the sun and twinkled like the stars in the sky. I never lost sight of her.

'Then I returned from the market one day and saw that she was shivering with cold. I was afraid. My daughter had a fever. I rubbed kernel oil on her and wrapped her up. In the night she developed a convulsion and died.'

'Ewo-o-o,' the people cried. 'So it happened,' some who knew the woman said.

'My only child died,' the woman went on. 'The world was in darkness for me. I wept like a human being, I wept like an animal. I threatened to jump into the grave and be buried alive with my only child. But I am still alive today. I have not had another baby since then. Have heart, my daughter. You are still young. It is still morning for you. So have heart.

100

We cannot explain the mysteries of life, because we are mere human beings. Only God knows. I am going.'

'That's it,' Ajanupu said. 'That's how to sympathize with a woman who has lost her only child. There are words of wisdom and encouragement. Efuru, you have heard what she said. So please have heart.'

Efuru nodded in assent.

Outside, people talked in whispers.

'Do you say that he is not home?' said one of the women.

'Don't you hear? He went to Ndoni with another woman and since then he has not come back. His mother has sent for him, but it will take two days for the message to get to him. If he comes home immediately, he will be here in four days.'

'Poor Efuru,' the other said. 'We all were surprised when she married that fool. And now see how shabbily she has been treated.'

'Do you think she is going to leave him?'

'You mean if Efuru would leave Adizua?'

'Yes.'

'I can't say. Efuru loves him very much and you know how we women love blindly. If he comes back to Efuru, I think she will forgive him. The problem is not that Efuru would not forgive him, it is that Adizua might not come back to her. It is in the family. Adizua's mother suffered at the hands of her husband just as Efuru is suffering.'

Woodcarving of a Yoruba mother with a child on her back.

ONE WIFE FOR ONE MAN

Frank Aig-Imoukhuede

Italicized line-by-line translation from West African
pidgin-English by Francis Ernest Kobina Parkes

I done try go to church, I done go for court.
I've tried the altar, I've tried the court-room.
Dem all dey talk about di 'new culture'.
All both of them talk about is this 'new culture'.
Dem talk about 'equality', dem mention 'divorce'.
They talk about 'equality' and proclaim 'divorce'.
Dem holler am so-tay my ear nearly cut;
They shout it so much my ear-drums nearly burst:
One wife for one man.

My fader before my fader get him wife barku.
My father's father had plenty of wives.
E no' get equality palaver; he live well.
He did all right without all this 'equality' humbug.
For he be oga for im own house.
And he was the boss in his own house.
Bot dat time done pass before white man come wit im
But since then the white man's come with this stuff about
One wife for one man.

Tell me how una woman no go make *yonga*
Tell me how a man can keep a woman from being bossy
Wen'e know say na 'im only dey.
When she knows well she has no lawful rival.
Suppose say-make God no 'gree-'e no born at all.
Suppose it is God's will she has no offspring at all.
A' tell you dat man bind dey craze wey start
I tell you the man must've been crazy who suggested
One wife for one man.

Jus' tell me how one wife fir do one man?
Just tell me how one wife can be enough for a man?
How man go fit stay all time for him house,
What can make a man stay home all the time
For when belle done kommotu.
When his one wife is pregnant as she can be?
How many pickin, self, one woman fir born

After all, how many children can one woman bear
When there's just one wife for one man?

Suppose self, say na so-so woman your wife dey born;
Suppose your wife's womb houses only females;
Suppose your wife sabe book, no' sabe make chop;
Suppose your wife is educated and doesn't know how to cook;
Den, how you go tell man make 'e no go out
Then how can you tell a man not to run around—
Sake of dis divorce? Bo, dis culture no waya o!
Or he'll be threatened by divorce. Man, this 'new culture' is awful:
Just one wife for one man!

ruba dish for food offerings,
presenting a female servant.

103

DANDA

(Excerpt)

Nkem Nwankwo

The scorch season was dying. The happiest time of the year, the season for feasts, when men and women laughed with all their teeth and little boys, their mouths oily oily, ran about the lanes blowing the crops of chicken to make balloons. In a few days the rain season would come and bring with it a ceaseless round of labour. And men would leave their homes with the first cry of the cock and would not return until the chicken came back to roost. Already the bushes were on fire and the acrid smell of burning permeated the earth.

Over the flames hovered the kite mourning the death of the year. In a few days he would flee the land to better places to escape the rain. But some people say that it is not the death of the scorch season that the kite mourns but the death of his mother. They tell how one day he culled pumpkin leaves from his farm and gave them to his mother to cook. But he hadn't known that pumpkin leaves shrink after they have been cooked. When his mother served him it, he was amazed by its smallness and in a fit of rage killed her. Then panicking he took the dead body and threw it into the flames of a bush fire. At the end of each scorch season, especially when he was hungry, he would remember his mother and go looking for her in the flames crying:

'Nnemu-o oku gbagbulu-u-u!'

Danda too did not look forward with eagerness to the coming of the rain season. But that night the moon was out and the night was fine. He determined to enjoy what remained of the season of the sun. So taking up his flute, he chirruped his favourite tunes up and down Aniocha.

The people in the surrounding villages had also come out to bid farewell to one half of the year. From Eziakpaka up the hill the warrior song trickled down as if from the sky. But before it reached Aniocha it had to filter through the huge forest at the boundary and eventually arrived from the bowels of the earth.

'Iye-e-e, eiye, eye!'

Everywhere Danda went there were exciting scenes. Women left their pots of bitter-leaf soup on the fire and stood tip-toe overlooking the outer walls of their compound. Children climbed ladders or orange trees and looked out. Dogs followed them and barked. The women called out:

'Rain, is there anything passing?'

'My wives, cook the bitter-leaf soup properly. I am coming right in.'

Bronze cast of the royal musician.

'That's it.' They clapped and cheered.

Danda fluted on. When he came to the compound of a man he was intimate with he called out that man's praise name. The responses of the men, depending on each person's character, were varied. Some remained in their obi and roared 'I hear'. Others burst out and looked over their walls and cried 'ewe ewe ewe!'

Danda came to the church premises and stood watching the tall ogbu trees. They had spread their arms and were rising up to the heavens. The moon too was coming down to meet them. Somewhere between the earth and the sky both met.

Danda fluted on inventing many variations to some well-known themes . . .

The Uwadiegwu umunna had gathered at the ogwe, a wooden stand rising in tiers, consisting of wooden benches placed on forked stakes. The men sat on the benches and snuffed. The women had formed a circle in an open square adjacent to the stands and were singing and clapping vigorously. A girl stood in the middle dancing the warrior dance and cutting through the air with the right hand in imitation of the slash of the matchet.

> 'Obulu nimalu aja.
> Gbuo nu mma ndi Agbaja
> Iye-e-e eiye eye.'

There was some colourful quality in the refrain which dispelled the spirit of darkness. For the night, even with the moon shining, has a heavy pressure that subdues the heart. But the song made the heart light and the eyes shine.

> 'Iye-e-e eiye eye
> Gbuo nu ma ndi Agbaja
> Iye—'

The song was interrupted by the entry of Danda. There was a roar of greeting.

'Rain! Is he drunk?'

'Daughters of beauty!' shouted Danda. 'All the men love you. If there is any man who doesn't love you let him put his head in the fire and see how he likes it. That song again, hou!' And accompanied by his oja the girls began the song of the Anambala canoemen. The dancer this time was Ekeama Idemmili the youngest wife of the chieftain. Laughing merrily, she flounced up and down. Her hands holding an imaginary paddle made the rhythmic motions of ploughing through the bubbling stream.

'Ugbom ana-a-a
Anambala
O na-a
Anambala.'

The men at the ogwe looked on, rapt in admiration.

'She is bright,' said a tapster.

'Bright, that's the word,' agreed Nwafo Ugo. 'I wonder from which village Nwokeke brought her. She is different from the women of these parts.'

'That was what I thought when first I saw her. I said to myself: this woman is not one of us.'

'No,' said Okelekwu waving his whip. 'She is from Umukrushe.'

'From where?'

'Umukrushe.'

There was a burst of laughter.

'Okelekwu, my brother, what did you say it was? People of our land wait a moment. Let the name reach the depths of my ear.'

'Umukrushe.'

'Ahai! The names that exist in this world!'

'But does it exist?' said the herdsman. 'Or is it just like a story?'

'It exists,' said Okelekwu, 'I have been there.' There was respectful silence. Okelekwu was a traveller. 'Yes,' he continued, 'when first I saw Ekeama I said to myself: "She is from Umukrushe." Then I asked Nwokeke and he said to me: "You are right." They have queer ways, those people. For instance the men do not pay bride price. Nwokeke paid nothing for Ekeama.'

'Then I will go there,' said Nwafo Ugo. 'What have I been waiting for? How long does it take to reach the place, Okelekwu?'

'Three days. You go in the land-boat.'

'Count me out,' said Nwafo. 'If I have to stay in a land-boat for three days I will be taken out in pieces.'

'But what I cannot understand is why they call themselves Umuku...'

'Umukrushe.'

'Call it whatever name you like. No village has the right to give itself such a name.'

'No,' said Nwafo, 'what interests me is that the people do not ask for bride price.'

'It is strange now that you should return to that point, Nwafo,' laughed the herdsman. 'Tell us the truth. What is wrong with your wife, Nwuka?'

'Yes, tell us!' roared the others. 'There is something inside your voice.'

'Well, every man wants to have one more wife if he can,' said Nwafo

107

a little lamely. 'How many of you would not like to fill your obi?'

'No,' said the herdsman. 'Who, with his eyes open, would want to cover himself with burning coals?'

The others laughed, some uneasily.

The singers had changed back to the warrior dance. Ekeama was at the moment demonstrating how the Agbaja warriors shot the arrow.

> 'Obulu ni mala Aja
> Gbaa nu uta ndi Agbaja
> Iye-e-e eiye eiye
> Gbuo nu mma ndi Agbaja—'

'You know what happened yesterday?' said Nwafo.

'What happened?' asked the herdsman smiling ironically.

'We were kneading mud for the new building of Okafo Nwalo. Then Ekeama dancing about and laughing and not looking which way she was going fell into the mud pit. She was not hurt but she could not climb out, the pit was deep. Danda was with us too—have I told you?— not in the pit but playing his oja outside. Then he saw the girl fall in. He stopped, leaned over the pit and lifted her up. But this is the one that will interest you—he did not let her down.'

'How do you mean?'

'She clung tightly to him, enclosed his head with her hands and pressed her face to his. With that hold he walked with her round the pit, and we laughed. Well, when he put her down do you know what she said? Ask me what she said. She said: "I do better than that in private".'

'Great woman,' said the herdsman.

The other men watched more attentively. Where Danda had succeeded they themselves shouldn't expect to fail.

'It is their way,' said Okelekwu. 'The women of her land are free. They are not stable. If you marry one of them today she may run off with another tomorrow.'

'Will her father return my bride price?'

'They have no bride price. I have just said so.'

'That's it. You see what happens when there is no bride price. So, Nwafo, do not go to your place, Umukulu—what's the horrid name again—to marry.'

'I will.'

'Go ahead. You will eat pepper.'

The night had gone far now, the moon itself looked weary and the air was becoming damp. The dancers had stopped and were dispersing. The men, too, rose and went. The ogwe was empty save for two people: Danda and Ekeama who for long afterwards whispered and made love under the cover of an ogbu tree.

Bronze plaque fixed in the Oba's columns, representing hunter shooting a bird.

108

THE MAN WITH THE UGLY WIFE

A Hausa legend

There was once a man who was married to a very plain wife, in fact the ugliest woman in the town. They were so poor that the husband had no decent gown to wear, the wife had no wraps, and they never had more than a day's food in the house.

One day the husband set about building a hut apart from the rest of the house. When he had finished he said to his wife: 'I'm going to go into this hut now and when I'm inside I want you to block up the entrance for me. I mean to live the life of a hermit for forty days and forty nights.'

When the man had shut himself up in the hut his wife sealed up the door with clay. He then spent all his days and nights in prayer and fasting. On the very last night of his vigil, however, he went to sleep and had a dream. In his dream he learnt that he could pray for three things and that whatever he prayed for would be granted to him.

Early next morning, as his time was up, he called to his wife to open the door and let him out. So she took a mattock and hacked down the clay wall which she had built over the door and released him. 'My prayers have been answered,' he said. 'For forty days and forty nights I prayed and fasted and on the last night of all I had a dream and in that dream it was revealed to me that I might pray for three things and that whatever I prayed for would be granted to me.'

When his wife had time to think about what he had told her she went to him and said: 'You know that I have no looks and am the ugliest woman in town and so I want you to pray for me to become beautiful.'

At nightfall the husband began to pray that the wife might become beautiful and, lo and behold, in the morning she had changed. She was now of surpassing softness and beauty so that in all the town there was not a woman to match her.

This news was soon carried to the palace. 'Indeed?' said the chief when he heard it. 'Well bring her here then. What are you waiting for?' So the woman was seized by force and carried off to the palace.

When the husband first discovered that he had lost his wife to the chief he was in despair. Later, however, he remembered that in all three prayers had been granted to him. He therefore prayed that his wife should be changed into a monkey.

Meanwhile in the palace the chief was just preparing to go to his new bride when his people came running in to tell him to go and see what had happened to her. The chief followed them to the woman's room and there instead of a bride he found a monkey sitting on the bed. He was very angry and ordered his slaves to take it away. They carried it to the husband's house and dumped it there.

When the husband found that his wife had indeed been changed into a monkey he prayed that she should be restored to her former self. His prayer was answered and she turned into the same ugly woman that she had been before.

Later the husband prayed for food and clothes and other things that he and his wife needed but his prayers were not answered because he had already used the three prayers which had been promised to him in his dream. 'In this world' he said to himself 'one thing is certain: any man who takes the advice of a woman will come to no good.'

THE JU-JU THAT WORKED

(Excerpt from The Overloaded Ark*)*

Gerald Durrell

The next two days were spent hunting with the dogs, and we had exceptionally good luck. The first day we caught a young Monitor and a full-grown Duiker, but it was on the second day that we secured a real prize. We had spent some hours rushing madly up and down the mountain following the dogs, who were following trails that seemed to lead nowhere, and at length we had halted for a rest among some huge boulders. We squatted on the rocks, gasping and sweating, while our dauntless pack lay at our feet, limp and panting. Soon, when we had all regained our breath somewhat, one of the dogs got up and wandered off into some neighbouring bushes, where we could hear it sniffing around, its bell clonking. Suddenly it let out a wild yelp, and we could hear it rushing off through the bushes; immediately the rest of the pack was galvanized into action and followed quickly with much yelping. We gathered up our things hastily, flung away our half-smoked cigarettes, and followed the pack with all speed. At first the trail led downhill, and we leapt wildly among the boulders and roots as we rushed down the steep incline. At one point there was a flimsy sapling hanging low over our path, and instead of ducking beneath it as the others had done, I brushed it aside with one hand. Immediately a swarm of black dots appeared before my eyes and an agonizing pain spread over my neck and cheek. On the branch which I had so carelessly thrust aside there was hanging a small forest wasps' nest, a thing the size of an apple hanging concealed beneath the leaves. The owners of these nests are swift and angry, and do not hesitate to attack, as I now realized. As I rushed on, clutching my cheek and neck and cursing fluently, it occurred to me that the hunters had seen the nest and had instinctively ducked to avoid disturbing it, and they presumably thought I would do the same. From then on I imitated their actions slavishly, while my head ached and throbbed.

It was the longest chase we had had to date; we must have run for nearly an hour, and towards the end I was so exhausted and in such pain that I did not really care if we captured anything or not. But eventually we caught up with the pack, and we found them grouped around the end of a great hollow tree trunk that stretched across the forest floor. The sight of the animal that crouched snarling gently at the dogs in the mouth of the trunk revived my interest in life immediately; it was the size of an English fox, with a heavy, rather bear-like face, and neat round ears. Its long sinuous body was cream coloured, as were its head and tail. Its slim and delicate legs were chocolate brown. It was a

112

Black-legged Mongoose, probably the rarest of the mongoose family in West Africa. On our arrival this rarity cast us a scornful glance and retreated into the interior of the trunk, and as soon as he had disappeared the dogs regained their courage and flung themselves at the opening and hurled abuse at him, though none of them, I noticed, tried to follow him.

The hunters now noticed for the first time that I had been stung, for my face and neck were swollen, and one eye was half closed in what must have looked like a rather lascivious wink. They stood around me moaning and clicking their fingers with grief, and ejaculating 'Sorry, sah!' at intervals, while the Tailor rushed off to a nearby stream and brought me water to wash the stings with. Application of a cold compress eased the pain considerably, and we then set about the task of routing the Mongoose from his stronghold. Luckily the tree was an old one, and under the crust of bark we found the wood dry and easy to cut. We laid nets over the mouth of the trunk, and then at the other end we cut a small hole and in this we laid a fire of green twigs and leaves. This was lit and the Tailor, armed with a great bunch of leaves, fanned it vigorously so that the smoke was blown along the hollow belly of the dead tree. As we added more and more green fuel to the fire, and the smoke became thicker and more pungent, we could hear the Mongoose coughing angrily inside the trunk. Soon it became too much for him, and he shot out into the nets in a cloud of smoke, like a small white cannon-ball from the mouth of a very large cannon. It took us a long time to unwind him, for he had tied himself up most intricately, but at last we got him into a canvas bag, and set off for camp, tired but in high spirits. Even the pain of my wasp stings was forgotten in the warm glow of triumph that enveloped me.

The next morning I awoke feeling wretched: my head ached, and my face was so swollen that I could hardly see out of my copiously watering eyes.

To irritate me still further it turned out to be one of N'da Ali's off days: she had enveloped herself in every available cloud and even the kitchen, a few paces away from the tent, was invisible in the white dampness. As I was gently masticating the remnants of my breakfast, Pious loomed out of the mist, and with him was a short, misshapen, evil-looking man bearing a huge basket on his head.

'Dis man bring beef, sah,' said Pious, eyeing my swollen face with disapproval.

The man bobbed and bowed, displaying withered yellow stumps of teeth in his fox's grin. I disliked him on sight, and I disliked him even more on opening his basket and finding inside, not the fine specimen I had hoped for, but a solitary mangy rat with an amputated tail. Having told the man what I thought of his beef I returned to my breakfast.

Pious and the man whispered together for a few minutes, the man glancing furtively at me now and then, and Pious came forward once more.

'Excuse me, sah, dis man come from Fineschang, and he say he get something to tell Masa.'

The man capered forward, bowing and grinning and flapping his wrinkled hands.

'Masa,' he whined, 'de people for Fineschang dey angry too much dat Masa done come for dis place. . . .'

'Well?'

'Yesterday dey done put *ju-ju* for Masa. . . .'

'Whar!' yelped Pious, slapping the man on the head so that his dirty hat fell over his eyes. 'Na what kind of *ju-ju* dey done put for Masa, ay?'

'No be bad *ju-ju*,' said the man hastily, 'only Masa no go catch any more beef for dis place, no go get lucky, get plenty rain too much, Masa no go stay.'

'Go tell the people of Fineschang I no fear their *ju-ju*,' I said wrathfully, 'I go stay here until I want to go, you hear? And if I see any Fineschang man for dis place, I get gun that get power too much, you hear, bush-man?'

'I hear, sah,' said the man, cringing, 'but why Masa de shout me, I no get palaver with Masa?'

'My friend, I savvay dis *ju-ju* talk: dis *ju-ju* no fit work if I no know dis ting, and so you be messenger boy, no be so?'

'No, sah, I no get palaver with Masa.'

'All right, now you go for Fineschang one time or I go get palaver with you. You hear?'

The man scuttled off through the mist and Pious gazed anxiously after him.

'You want I go beat him, sah?' he asked hopefully.

'No, leave him.'

'Eh! I no like dis *ju-ju* business, sah.'

'Well, don't tell the others, I don't want them all panicky.'

It was the first time that I have had a *ju-ju* put on me, and I was interested to see what would happen. I most emphatically do not dismiss *ju-ju* as a lot of nonsense and mumbo-jumbo, and anyone who does so is a fool, for *ju-ju* is a very real and potent force all over Africa, and has been known to produce results which are difficult to explain away. Perhaps the commonest sort, and the most effective, is where you have the co-operation of your victim. By this I mean that the man must *know* he has had a *ju-ju* placed on him, and then, if he believes in magic, he is ripe for the slaughter. A 'well-wisher' comes to the unfortunate man and tells him that a *ju-ju* has been placed on him, and then, if he believes it, he is left in horrid suspense for a time. Slowly the whole

114

plot is unfolded to him by different 'well-wishers' (these, in Africa, are just as deadly as their European counterparts) and he learns that he is gradually to waste away and die. If he is sufficiently convinced of the efficacy of the spell, he *will* waste away and die. The man who had just been to see me was one of these 'well-wishers', and now that I had been told about the *ju-ju*, it was more or less up to me. The curious thing was that the *ju-ju did* work, better than anyone could have wished, but how much of it was due to my own unconscious efforts, and how much was mere coincidence, I don't know.

Ceremonial bronzes of Upper Nigeria, used for magic and divination.

THE ANIMALS' FARM

A Hausa legend

The elephant once mustered the other animals and said to them: 'Now all of you, whoever you may be, come here because we are going to make a farm.'

'Very well,' said the animals.

'You must live on the job,' said the elephant, 'and put in a week's work.'

'Very well,' said the animals. The hyena went along with the rest of them and they began to clear a farm.

They worked with a will and when the week was up the elephant said that he would go and see what they had done. But when he arrived he found that they had not cleared very much, no more than a man could cross in a couple of hours' march. This made him very angry and he began pushing over trees himself. He kept pushing them over and pushing them over until the clearing stretched away a day's march in every direction.

When the rains came the animals went out again and began drilling holes for the seed. The field-mouse kept tumbling into the holes, which he could not get out of, and shouting 'Ho there up front! Stop digging pits for us at the back to fall into.' But the others carried on until the whole farm was sown and then they went home.

When it was time for the hoeing they turned out again and hoed the whole farm. Next, when the corn had ripened, they went out again and cut it. Then they built a corn-bin and harvested their corn and closed up the bin. 'Now animals,' said the elephant, 'gather round so that I can talk to you. We will go on eating herbage for the present and leave our corn in the bin until the hot weather.'

'Very well,' said the animals and went their different ways.

But the rabbit said to himself that he would go into the scrub and lie low until all the others had gone. When the coast was clear he went back to the corn-bin and helped himself. Afterwards he went and got some of the hyena's droppings and put them in the bin. He went on doing this until it was time for the other animals to return.

When the others came back from their dry-season expeditions they all assembled again. The only one who was not there was the rabbit and he was in the scrub, lying low. When they called to him, shouting 'Ho Zomo!' he only answered faintly.

'Zomo must have gone a long way,' said the animals to one another. 'Hark how faintly he answers when we call.' Each time they shouted 'Ho Zomo!' he answered, but still only faintly. But at last he dashed up, showering them with earth and dust, and they saw that he was panting so much that his tongue was hanging out.

'Now then,' said the elephant, 'are we all present?'

'All present,' said the camel.

The animals said that the rabbit should go and look into the corn-bin but the hyena said that he would go. So he climbed up but when he looked inside and saw that there was nothing there, only some of his own droppings, he said, 'Ah! Ah!! Ah!!!'.

'What's the matter?' said the animals.

'I swear it wasn't me,' said the hyena.

The animals said that the rabbit should go and have a look. So the rabbit climbed up on the corn-bin and looked inside and said, 'It's full of the hyena's droppings.'

This made the elephant very cross and he went to open the bin himself but only stove it in.

'I swear it wasn't me,' said the hyena again.

'Well, whoever it was,' said the elephant, 'I am going to find him. Let everyone go and put on a loin-cloth.'

So all the animals went and made loin-cloths. The hyena's was plain but the rabbit made a fancy one out of hemp. He put this on and went and danced about in front of the hyena.

'Some people have all the luck,' said the hyena. 'Will you swap?'

'There you are,' said the rabbit, giving the hyena his fancy loin-cloth and taking the plain one instead.

'Now go and collect firewood,' said the elephant. So the animals went off and collected firewood and built a fire and set a light to it.

When the fire was burning the elephant jumped over it. 'Whoever fails to jump over the fire,' he said, 'is the one who has done this mischief.'

So all the animals jumped over the fire. The giraffe jumped over, the bush-cow jumped over, and the rabbit jumped over. But when it came to the hyena, his loin-cloth caught on fire.

'Beat him,' cried all the animals. With that they all laid into him and the elephant gave him such a thump that his rump sagged. That is why he now looks as if he is squatting down even when he is standing up.

THE GROUND SQUIRREL AND THE LION

A Hausa legend

The animals once realized that the lion was killing them all off.

'Look here' they said to one another 'if we want to live we must make a plan. Otherwise the lion will put an end to us all.'

So they had a meeting and when they had finished they went in a body to see the lion.

'Lords of the Jungle' they said when they had found him 'we have come to ask a favour of you. If every morning we bring one of our number to you to eat, we want you to leave the rest of us alone.'

'Very well' said the lion.

The animals therefore went away and drew lots. The first lot fell on the gazelle and so the others seized him and took him to the lion. The lion ate him and was satisfied and did not go hunting again that day.

Next morning the animals drew lots again and this time the lot fell on the roan antelope. He too was seized and taken to the lion and eaten.

So it went on until one day the lot fell on the ground-squirrel. The other animals seized him and were about to take him to the lion when he stopped them. 'No' he said 'set me free and I'll go to the lion by myself.' The other animals agreed to this and let him go.

When he was free the ground-squirrel retired to his hole and slept until midday. Meanwhile the lion, who had not had his usual meal and had therefore become very hungry, was roaming about the bush and roaring and trying to find something to eat. At length the squirrel came out of his hole and climbed a tree near the well.

The squirrel waited there in the tree until the lion came past and then he asked him what he was roaring about.

'What am I roaring about?' asked the lion. 'Why, ever since early morning I've been waiting for you people and you haven't brought me a thing.'

'Well, it was like this' said the squirrel 'we drew lots and the lot fell on me. I was on my way to you with a bowl of honey which you would have enjoyed when another lion met me by the well over there and took the honey away from me by force.'

'Where is this other lion?' asked the lion.

'He's down the well' said the squirrel. 'But he's stronger than you are' he added.

The lion became very angry when he heard this. He dashed over to the well and stood at its mouth and looked down inside. There he thought he saw the other lion looking up at him and so he swore at him.

Silence. He swore at him again. Still silence. His rage now got the better of him and he sprang at the other lion and fell into the well and was drowned.

The squirrel then went back to the other animals. 'I've killed the lion' he said 'so now you can all live your lives as you please. But as for me' he went on 'I'm going to retire to my hole again.'

'Strategy is better than strength' cried all the other animals. 'The squirrel has killed the lion.'

INVOCATION OF THE CREATOR

A Yoruba legend translated by Ulli Beier

He is patient, he is not angry.
He sits in silence to pass judgement.
He sees you even when he is not looking.
He stays in a far place—but his eyes are on the town.

He stands by his children and lets them succeed.
He causes them to laugh—and they laugh.
Ohoho—the father of laughter.
His eye is full of joy.
He rests in the sky like a swarm of bees.

Obatala—who turns blood into children.

NOTES ON AUTHORS and FURTHER READING

CHINUA ACHEBE, born in 1930, was one of the first graduates of University College, Ibadan. His father was a mission teacher. After a visit to America he joined the Nigerian Broadcasting Corporation in 1954, and when he resigned in 1967 he was Director of External Broadcasting. He is now on the staff of the Institute of African Studies at the University of Nigeria at Nsukka. His first novel, *Things Fall Apart*, was published in 1958. Other novels include *No Longer at Ease* (1960), *Arrow of God* (1964), *A Man of the People* (1966).

FRANK AIG-IMOUKHUEDE was born in 1935 at Edunabon, near Ife, though his home is in Benin Province. While at University College, Ibadan, he contributed poetry to J. P. Clark's *The Horn*. Two of his poems have appeared in *Black Orpheus*, and he was the first of the young Nigerian poets to attempt writing in pidgin English. He has written plays for broadcasting, and is an Information Officer at Ibadan.

WILLIAM ALLEN (1793–1864) took part in the Niger expeditions of 1832 and 1841–2, and published, together with T. H. R. Thomson, *A Narrative of the expedition sent by Her Majesty's Government to the River Niger in 1841* (London 1848). Captain Allen was in charge of the *Wilberforce*, the ship that was used by the expedition, and he was also responsible for the surveying. His sketches and paintings provide an invaluable visual record of Nigerian life in that period.

BABA of KARO (ca 1883–1951) was a Hausa woman who lived in the Nigerian states of Kano and Zaria from 1890 until her death. Her father belonged to the Kanuri people, from Kukawa, the nineteenth-century capital of Bornu. She related her autobiography to Mrs M. F. Smith, who translated it.

ULI BEIER is Director of the Institute of African Studies in the University of Ife. While he was editor of *Black Orpheus* and an associate professor in the Department of Extra-Mural Studies in the University of Ibadan, Beier became known for his outstanding translations from the Yoruba, as well as for his books on African art and literature. He was one of the editors of *Modern Poetry from Africa* in the Penguin African Library, and his books include *Political Spider*, *Not Even God is Ripe Enough*, *The Origin of Life and Death*, and a book on Yoruba Poetry.

ADOLPHE EURDO was born in Liège, Belgium, in 1849, and died in Paris in 1891. In 1878 he sailed for the Niger, which he explored for the International African Association. He subsequently visited East Africa and the area east of Lake Tanganyika. *The Niger and the Benueh* was published in London in 1880.

SIR RICHARD BURTON (1821–1890) went abroad at an early age with his parents, the prelude to a life of travel and adventure. In 1840 he matriculated at Trinity College, Oxford, but did not graduate; in the course of his travels, however, he mastered 35 languages, and in 1849 published three works on philology relating to Asian languages. Already he had served as a cadet in the Indian army, and had gained an intimate knowledge of Muhammedan manners in his wanderings. In 1853 he made a pilgrimage to Mecca. In 1855 he served in the Crimea, and the following year was second in command to Speke on the expedition to discover the sources of the Nile. In 1860 he went to North America, and married. 1861–5 he was British consul at Fernando Po, from where he was able to visit the Nigerian coast. He was subsequently consul in Damascus and Trieste, and devoted his later years to literature and a translation of the Arabian Nights. These passages are from *Wanderings in West Africa*, London, 1863.

HUGH CLAPPERTON (1788–1827) started as a cabin boy in 1801, was press-ganged for the navy, and was a midshipman in the East Indies from 1808–13. He was in Canada from 1814–17. He travelled to Nigeria in 1822, and became a commander in the Royal Navy. He was again in Nigeria from 1825–7, and died near Sokota. Accounts of his travels were published by his companions, Dixon Denham and Richard Lander.

JOHN PEPPER CLARK was born in the Ijaw country of the Niger Delta in 1935. In 1960 he graduated from University College, Ibadan, where he founded a poetry magazine, *The Horn*. He visited America on a fellowship and has since lectured at Lagos University. As well as several poems in *Black Orpheus* he has written plays, *Song of a Goat* (1961), *The Masquerade*, *The Raft*, and *Ozidi* (1966), and a book of reportage *America, their America* (Andre Deutsch, London, 1964). In 1965 he published a volume of poetry, *A Reed in the Tide* (Longmans, London).

DIXON DENHAM (1786–1828) served in the Peninsular war, and received the Waterloo medal in 1815. He volunteered to explore the country between

Timbuctoo and the North coast of Africa. In 1823 he took part in inter-tribal warfare, and the following year partially explored Lake Chad. In 1825 a post was specially created for him to supervise the liberated Africans on the West coast. He died Lieutenant Governor of Sierra Leone. *Narrative of Travels and Discoveries in Northern and Central Africa in the Years 1822, 1823, and 1824,* which included the collaboration of Commander Clapperton, was published in London in 1826, and the *Journal of a Second Expedition into the Interior of Africa from the Bight of Benin to Soccatoo, to which is added the journal of Richard Lander from Kano to the sea-coast,* was published in London, 1829.

GERALD DURRELL was born in India in 1925. From 1946 onwards he made expeditions to little-known parts of the world, and collected for all the major zoos. His books include *The Overloaded Ark, A Zoo in My Luggage, The Bafut Beagles, The Drunken Forest, My Family and Other Animals, Three Singles to Adventure,* and *Encounters with Animals.*

CYPRIAN EKWENSI was born in Minna, Northern Nigeria, in 1921. Educated in Ibadan, Ghana and at London University, where he studied pharmacy, he taught chemistry in Nigeria before joining the Nigerian Broadcasting Corporation. Subsequently he became Director of Information in the Federal Ministry of Information, but he has now retired and gone into business on his own. He has written novels, short stories and children's books, including *People of the City* (1954), *Jagua Nana* (1961), *An African Night's Entertainment* (1962), *Burning Grass* (1962), *Beautiful Feathers* (1963), *Iska* (1966) and *Lokotown* (1966).

OLAUDAH EQUIANO was born in 1745 in Essaka. He was kidnapped from his home in Iboland during a slave raid in 1756. He was transported in a slave ship to Virginia, and later to England, where he was sold to Captain Henry Pascal who named his Gustavus Vassa. He was able to purchase his freedom in 1766 and for the next ten years continued to sail in merchant ships to different parts of the world. He tried, unsuccessfully, to be sent as a missionary to Africa, and took an active role in the anti-slave movement, petitioning the Queen in 1788 on behalf of his fellow Africans.

ADEBAYO FALETI is a Yoruba poet who specialises in Nigerian folklore. He has worked as a script-writer on the staff of Television House in Ibadan. His poem 'Independence' won First Award for Yoruba Literature in the 1957 Nigeria Festival of Arts.

MARY KINGSLEY (1862–1900) was daughter of the traveller George Kingsley, author of the *South Sea Bubble*, and niece of Charles Kingsley, the novelist. From 1893–4 she visited the West coast of Africa, the Congo River and old Calabar, and made valuable zoological collections together with her notes and observations. Her *Travels in West Africa; Congo Français, Corisco and Cameroons*, published in London in 1897, may be regarded as the first of the West African anthropological studies. Miss Kingsley sought to understand African society as a thing apart. She died while nursing Boer prisoners in South Africa in 1900.

MACGREGOR LAIRD (1807–1861) was the younger son of the famous Birkenhead shipbuilder William Laird. In *Narrative of an Expedition into the Interior of Africa by the River Niger in 1832–4* (London 1837) Laird describes the expedition with Oldfield made in his 55-ton paddle steamer *Alburka*.

RICHARD LANDER (1804–34) accompanied Hugh Clapperton to West Africa in 1822 and in 1830–31 he attempted to explore the Niger, making a second expedition in 1832. He was mortally wounded in a fight with tribes at Ingiamma and died at Fernando Po. The course and outlet of the Niger was settled by his exploration. In 1832 he published *Journal of an Expedition to explore the Course and Termination of the Niger*, together with his brother John Lander.

FREDERICK LUMLEY was born in Edinburgh, Scotland in 1927. He first travelled in Africa in 1948, when he was a student at the University of Edinburgh, visiting Kano, the former Belgian Congo, and Nyasaland, known today as Malawi. After a period in journalism, when he was literary editor of the *Weekly Scotsman* he went into publishing in London in 1958, where as reader and adviser he became familiar with the work of a number of young African novelists who were subsequently published. Mr Lumley is himself author of a book which has become a standard work on the modern theatre, *New Trends in 20th Century Drama*, originally published 1958, latest edition 1971.

JOHN MUNONYE was born in 1929 in Akokwa and educated at Christ the King College, Onitsha, and as a postgraduate at London University. For the last twenty years he has been a civil servant in the Ministry of Education. At the moment he is Principal of the Advanced Teacher Training College at Owerri. His first two novels were *The Only Son*, and *Obi* (1969), and he has since written *Oil Man of Obange* and *A Wreath for the Maidens* (1973).

NKEM NWANKWO was born in 1936. He was educated at Lagos and University College, Ibadan. He has worked for the Nigerian Broadcasting Corporation, and his novel *Danda* has been adapted for the stage.

FLORA NWAPA was born in 1931 and brought up at Oguta in Eastern Nigeria. She is a graduate of the University College, Ibadan, and in 1958 took a diploma in education at Edinburgh University. Returning to Nigeria, she has been a Woman Education Officer, Assistant Registrar (University of Lagos) and after the war she was appointed Commissioner for Health and Social Welfare in the East Central State. She has published two novels, *Efuru* (1966) and *Idu* (1969).

ONUORA NZEKWU was born in 1928 at Kafanchan, Northern Nigeria. He taught for several years before becoming a journalist. He has published three novels, *Wand of Noble Wood* (1961), *Blade Among the Boys* (1962) and *High Life for Lizards* (1966).

GABRIEL OKARA was born in 1921 in Bumodi. Educated in Umuahia, Nigeria, and in North-Western University in America, where he studied journalism. Until 1967 he was Information Officer with the Eastern Regional Government at Enugu. His poems have appeared in *Black Orpheus*. His novel *The Voice* was published by Andre Deutsch, London, 1964.

CHRISTOPHER OKIGBO was born in 1932 at Ojoto near Onitsha in the Ibo country of Eastern Nigeria; he died in 1967 on the Nsukka battlefield. Educated at Government College, Umuahia, and University College, Ibadan (where he read classics) he was, from 1956–8 Private Secretary to the Federal Minister of Research and Information, and later joined the library staff at the University of Nigeria. He has published *Heavensgate* (Mbari, Ibadan, 1962), *Limits* (Mbari, Ibadan, 1964), *Silences* in *Transition* No 8 (1963), *Distances* in *Transition* No 16, *Lament for the Drums* part II (Mbari 1965) and *Path of Thunder* in *Black Orpheus*, February 1968.

MUNGO PARK (1771–1806), born near Selkirk in Scotland, he studied medicine in Edinburgh. He served as a surgeon in the merchant marine and visited Sumatra, and attracted interest on his return with his botanical and zoological collection. In 1795 he joined the African Association, and made a voyage to discover the Niger. In 1799 he published the results of this in *Travels in the Interior of Africa*. In 1805 he accepted the government invitation made by Lord Camden to undertake another journey to discover the source of the Nile. He is thought to have been killed by hostile tribes.

FRANCESCA YETUNDE PEREIRA was born in 1933 in Lagos. After graduating from University College, London in 1959, she returned to Nigeria to join the Federal Service as an administrative officer attached to the Cabinet. Apart from her poems, she has also written short stories and has made her mark as a folk singer—in 1961 she appeared at the American Society of African Culture Festival of the Arts, accompanied on the guitar by Wole Soyinka.

WOLE SOYINKA was born in 1935 at Abeokuta in the Yoruba country of Western Nigeria, the son of a school's supervisor. He was educated at Ibadan University and Leeds, where he took English Honours. For the following 18 months he studied theatre in London and his first play *The Invention* was produced at the Royal Court Theatre. In 1960 he returned to Nigeria where his verse play *A Dance of the Forests* was produced for Nigerian Independence in October 1960. *The Road* won first prize at the Dakar Festival of Negro Arts, 1960. In 1964 *Five Plays* was published by the Oxford University Press, and in 1965 Andre Deutsch published his novel *The Interpreters*. *The Man Died* (1972), *A Shuttle in the Crypt* (poems), a play *Madmen and Specialists* (1971), and a novel *Season of Anomy* (1973) form a quartet designed as an expression of the affirmative humane response to chaos and blind social forces. *The Bacchae*, an adaptation of Euripedes, was commissioned by the National Theatre of Great Britain.

AMOS TUTUOLA was born of Christian parents in Abeokuta. Tutuola left school early and worked as a copper-smith, a government messenger and later store-keeper with the Nigerian Broadcasting Service in Ibadan. His first novel, *The Palm-Wine Drinkard* (1952), was followed by *Feather Woman of the Jungle*, *My Life in the Bush of Ghosts*, *Simbi and the Satyr of the Dead Jungle*, and *Ajaiya and His Inherited Poverty* (1967).

TEXT ACKNOWLEDGMENTS

The editor and publishers are grateful for permission to include in this anthology works by the following:

Chinua Achebe, excerpt from *Things Fall Apart*, published by William Heinemann Ltd;

Frank Aig-Imoukhuede, 'One Wife for One Man', reprinted from *Poems from Black Africa*, ed. Langston Hughes, copyright © 1963, by permission of Indiana University Press, Bloomington;

Ulli Beier, 'Invocation of the Creator' from *African Poetry*, published by Cambridge University Press, 1966;

John Pepper Clark, 'Agbor Dancer', reprinted from *Poems from Black Africa*, ed. Langston Hughes, copyright © 1963, by permission of Indiana University Press, Bloomington;

Gerald Durrell, excerpt from *The Overloaded Ark*, reprinted by permission of Faber and Faber Ltd;

Cyprian Ekwensi, 'The Girls from Lagos' from *Iska*, published by Hutchinson Publishing Group Ltd;

Adebayo Faleti, 'Independence', reprinted from *Poems from Black Africa*, ed. Langston Hughes, copyright © 1963, by permission of Indiana University Press, Bloomington;

H. A. S. Johnston, three stories from *A Selection of Hausa Stories* © 1966 Oxford University Press, reprinted by permission of The Clarendon Press, Oxford;

John Munonye, excerpt from *A Wreath for the Maidens*, published by Heinemann Educational Books Ltd;

Nkem Nwanko, excerpt from *Danda*, first published by Andre Deutsch, 1964, copyright © 1964 Nkem Nwankwo;

Flora Nwapa, excerpt from *Efuru*, published by Heinemann Educational Books Ltd;

Onuora Nzekwu, excerpt from *High Life for Lizards*, published by Hutchinson Publishing Group Ltd;

Gabriel Okara, 'Piano and Drums', reprinted from *Poems from Black Africa*, ed. Langston Hughes, copyright © 1963, by permission of Indiana University Press, Bloomington;

Christopher Okigbo, 'Lament of the Drums' from *Labyrinths*, published by Heinemann Educational Books Ltd;

Francesca Yetunde Pereira, 'Two Strange Worlds' and 'The Paradox', reprinted from *Poems from Black Africa*, ed. Langston Hughes, copyright © 1963, by permission of Indiana University Press, Bloomington;

Mary Smith, excerpt from *Baba of Karo*, reprinted by permission of Faber and Faber Ltd;

Wole Soyinka, 'Abiku', reprinted from *Poems from Black Africa*, ed. Langston Hughes, copyright © 1963, by permission of Indiana University Press, Bloomington; and excerpt from *The Interpreters*, first published by Andre Deutsch, 1965, copyright © 1965 Wole Soyinka;

Amos Tutuola, excerpt from *The Palm-Wine Drinkard*, reprinted by permission of Faber and Faber Ltd.

The publishers would like to thank all the copyright-holders, museums, galleries and private collectors, who have given permission to Werner Forman to photograph the material reproduced in this book.

Academy of Sciences collection, Leningrad: 58

Benin City Museum: 77

Trustees of the British Museum, London: 10, 28, 47, 57, 61, 107

Collection Alan Brandt, New York: 37

Collection John Friede, New York: 69, 103

Collection Phillip Goldmann, London: 65, 67, 74, 75, 78, 101, 115

Mansell Collection, London: 30, 31

Trenchard Gallery of Art, University of Ibadan: 40

Staatliches Museum für Völkerkunde, Berlin: 73, 111

Photographs by other photographers: © Dr. Georg Gerster-John Hillelson Agency, London: 49. © Nigeria Government Information Office, Lagos: 70 and back endpapers. © George Rodger, MAGNUM: 53. © Marc Riboud, MAGNUM: 88.

If any persons with rights or interests in these publications has not been acknowledged, the omission is entirely unintentional and very much regretted.